2/7/13

To Bill,

Service,

+

Humility,

=

Winning!

Thanks For Your Support..

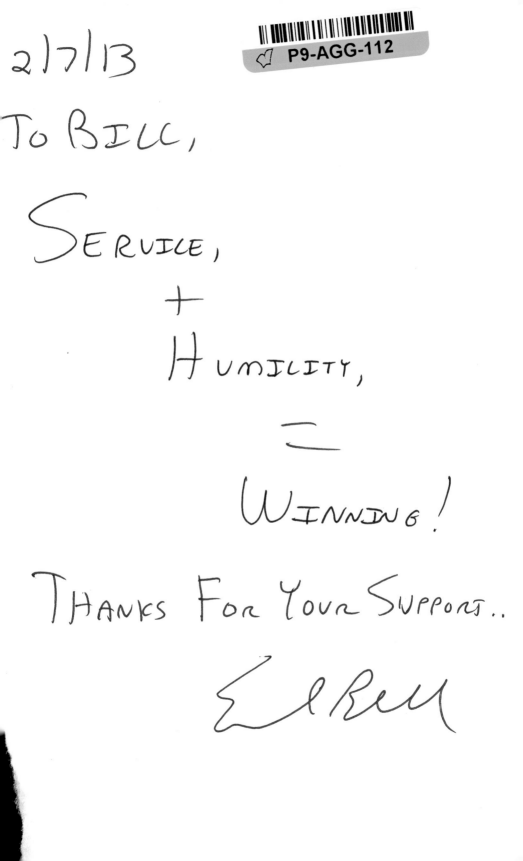

More Praise For
Winning in Baseball and Business

"Anyone wanting to grow and improve his company should read Earl Bell's book, Winning in Baseball and Business, which takes the reader on a 10-inning journey that will transform his business—its company mission, culture, leadership team, employees, and systems—into a fine-tuned moneymaking machine. Behind each inning are workshop exercises that will help change the relationship between an owner and his business from self-jobbed to self-supported. The outcome of this work is a growing, sustainable, and profitable business that gives its owners more discretionary time."

— **Mark Walters, Lawyer, Business Strategist, Trusted Advisor, General Counsel to Go, www.generalcounseltogo.com**

"Winning in Baseball and Business is a fun read, easy to understand, and inspiration-al. I really appreciated how Mr. Bell focused on the essential few things that must be done right if you want to build a thriving company. My partner and I started a company and grew it to $250 million in annualized billings using many of these same principles. I heartily recommend this book to anyone starting or trying to grow a company."

— **Ron Elgin, Retired Chairman and CEO, DDB Seattle**

"One of the real truisms of business is that it mirrors sports. Or maybe it's the other way around! Regardless, the business world learns valuable lessons from the world of sports, especially baseball. Earl Bell is an expert in both. As a baseball coach, he has guided young men and women to achieve on the field of play, while learning lessons in sportsmanship and character building. In the same way, Earl works with business executives to grow their business and effectively plan and strategize for long-term results. In this book, he has used baseball as the vehicle to help you grow faster and stronger!"

— **Dan Weedin, President, Toro Consulting Inc., www.danweedin.com**

"Earl Bell has put together a very concise, readable, and valuable book on growing your business. Beyond the typical pep-talk that self-help efforts normally put forth, this book takes you on a journey that, in my experience, will produce results. Read it, do it—profit from it."

— **Wayne Willich, Retired Executive, The Boeing Company**

"Like most things, the key ideas and skills in Winning in Baseball and Business are simple, and for most of us, not that easy. What I especially like about this book is that it is playful, just like any good game of baseball. Have fun, practice, and develop your skills. By the third inning of Earl Bell's book, you may begin to see what is special about Earl and why this book reads so well. Like Earl, Winning in Baseball and Business is clear, focused, and full of gold."

— **Dave Shapiro, CEO, Excell Puget Sound,**
www.excellpugetsound.com

"Everything I needed to succeed in business I learned from playing sports as a kid. Let's face it—athletes have an unfair advantage in the marketplace because of our foundation of learning the importance of discipline, teamwork, and perseverance. If you want to take your business to the next level, then read this book and rediscover the principles your coach taught you as a kid, that will deliver big results for your business now as an adult!"

— **Patrick Snow, International Best-Selling Author of *Creating Your Own Destiny***
and *The Affluent Entrepreneur*, www.PatrickSnow.com

"When you first meet Earl Bell and see that energized twinkle in his eye, you know immediately there is something special about this business consultant, entrepreneur, & Little League "Casey Stengel." In Winning in Baseball and Business, Earl brings a renewed sense of the strategic importance to words like Vision, Mission, Values—a sharp contrast to the "consultant speak" that permeates so much of today's business literature. In today's world where customers are looking for value, business owners for profitability, and employees for meaningful connections and collaboration, Earl's narrative on the transferable experiences between baseball and business, are both simple and profound. Embracing big visions, realizing aspirations, thinking and acting on what "could be"—all are here in this informative journey. A must-read for business owners in pursuit of their dreams."

— Scott Harrison, CEO/Owner, BarclayDean Environments, www.BarclayDean.com

"If you played a sport as a youth, you remember that one coach who taught you not only the fundamentals of the game, but also teamwork, perseverance, personal responsibility, and ethics—all essential skills for success. Using baseball metaphors, Earl walks the reader through the many challenges facing today's entrepreneur. This is not your typical "self-help" book that uses dated and standardized formulas, but rather, its fresh approach provides a practical and concise roadmap, and its application will help solidify the necessary traits the reader will require for success."

— Steven A. Rhone, Founder, Rhone Asset Management

"Companies often recruit potential employees who have an athletic background because athletics help prepare people for the corporate world. The lessons learned in athletics—teamwork, overcoming adversity, work ethic, etc. are applicable in the business world. Now, Earl Bell, in his outstanding book, Winning in Baseball and Business: Transforming Little League Principles into Major League Profits for Your Company shows how a business leader can take lessons learned on the baseball field and translate them to use in the business world. This book is a vital resource for executives who want to grow their business to greater profitability."

— Michael Butler, Chairman and CEO, Cascadia Capital LLC, www.CascadiaCapital.com

"Earl has really "hit it out of the ball park" with this book. He provides entrepreneurs with both the questions they need to answer to be successful and the stories of the people who've been successful by answering them clearly and intentionally. It provides a simple and compelling road map for how to start and create a business by design versus by default. I've worked with dozens of entrepreneurs. The ones who are most successful are those who take the time up-front to answer questions like these and then use those answers to build the business of their dreams."

— Alison Whitmire, CEO/Entrepreneur Coach, C-lever Biz, www.c-lever.biz

"Having authored a book of my own, I realize the importance of "connecting" with your readers so they can easily understand and grasp the concepts. Without this, the value of the information is never realized. Earl has done a masterful job of "connecting" with the reader in such a way that you can't wait to see what comes next. Many books also never get beyond the "concept" stage and don't offer the necessary steps to put them into action—Earl also eliminated this issue by offering valuable worksheets so you can put the lessons into practice immediately. The comparatives to baseball (which are also transferable to many other sports) make this an easy read with high value. I can't wait to share this book with my friends and colleagues—a definite positive addition to anyone's library!"

— Blaine Millet, President and Chief Advocate, WOM10,
www.WOM10.com

"Earl Bell has made an incredible impact on my business and how I view team building. Growing up playing athletics at a competitive level and transitioning into a business owner gave me a great appreciation for Earl's book. It made me appreciate the business coach he is even more, but it also made me wish I had him as an athletic coach growing up. I highly recommend reading Winning in Baseball and Business and working with Earl to grow value in your business."

— Lucas Mack, Owner, 4th Avenue Media,
www.4thAvenueMedia.com

"Earl always talks about working ON your business so I'm very pleased to see that he has weaved his love of baseball in a clear and concise "how to" book for business owners. What keeps me up at night are some of the things that Earl so clearly asks us to answer about our own businesses. This is not a onetime read but rather a book to refer to and revisit. Thanks, Earl!"

— Rick Page, Commercial Real Estate Broker, Office Lease,
www.OfficeLease.com

"If you are serious about transforming your business, and by default your life, Earl has just provided you with an invaluable roadmap. From my own exploration about why I started Highland, I've noted a significant increase in energy and passion when aligned with values and a healthy culture. This book offers more than Little League ideas—it instead provides Major League secrets to business success."

— **John Christianson, Founder & CEO, Highland Private Wealth Management, www.HighlandPrivate.com**

"Earl's passion for helping business owners comes across clearly. Within two months, he has given me ideas that have instantly improved my business, not only by increasing profitability but most importantly, my staff is working better together than they ever have before.... Winning in Baseball and Business is a must-read."

— **Jose Rijo-Berger, President, Rijo Athletics, Public and Motivational Speaker, Professional Scout for the St. Louis Cardinals, www.RijoAthletics.com**

"Whether it is a 9-inning game or an extended season, baseball is a blend of intuition, mental preparation, physical stamina, and proper execution. Experts say no sport takes more coordination and skill than does baseball. Running a successful business takes a successful blend of intuition, mental preparation, physical stamina, and proper execution too. There couldn't be a better way to help learn to do better business than by learning how to do better baseball. Earl has found the perfect teaching tool."

— **Rich Budke, President, Trutina Financial, www.TrutinaFinancial.com**

"A good leader knows that teams matter. And as a person who has had the privilege of being on a team led by Earl Bell, I know that the team-building principles in this book can absolutely work for strengthening your organization."

— **James Whitfield, President, Leadership Eastside, www.LeadershipEastside.com**

"A clever title for a pithy book—one that reads with a zest and verve I would expect from Earl Bell. Earl is the master of metaphor in this delightfully readable tome of sound advice—for growing your business, for building a winning team, for living a more dynamic life. Earl's voice in Winning in Baseball and Business is passionate, witty, and engaging. A fun and compelling read."

— **Bill Weis, Professor of Management, Seattle University, www.seattleu.edu/albers**

"Sports analogies have been tied to business in many successful books. This one is distinctive in the storytelling style and the practical exercises tied together with compelling suggestions. A quick read that will create some pause and reflection. Fresh reminders and crisp connections make it a worthy read."

— Debbie Wardrop, General Manager, The Resort at Port Ludlow, www.PortLudlowResort.com

"With Winning in Baseball and Business, Earl Bell has delivered a trifecta: Easy to read, easy to understand, and easy to implement. Earl's straightforward approach and no-nonsense game plan make this a must-read. You will be glad you did read it!"

— Mitch Mounger, CEO, Sunrise Identity, www.sunriseid.com

"As a businesswoman, I sometimes pretend that I don't really do sports metaphors, but in reality, I've been an athlete all my life. Earl Bell's Winning in Baseball and Business shares the simple, essential reminders about what we need for success, the first of which is to step up to the plate. It's not just about showing up to our companies and teams; it's about our full presence, commitment, and the heart it takes to win. Bell's book will have you ready for that first pitch!"

— Libby Wagner, poet and president of Libby Wagner & Associates and author of Amazon best-selling *The Influencing Option: The Art of Building a Profit Culture in Business*, www.LibbyWagner.com

"I have the utmost appreciation and respect for Earl Bell and his passion to help business owners and executives move from good to great. Whether your business has $2 million in sales or $200 million in sales, you have much to gain as Earl shares his wisdom and stories of winners and losers in both baseball and business. I would encourage any business owner or executive to apply Earl's principles wholeheartedly and expeditiously."

— John O'Dore, Managing Director, Meridian Capital, www.MeridianLLC.com

"Finally! A book designed to provide real, practical, AND implementable actions designed to increase the profitability and value of your company. Winning in Baseball and Business utilizes the world of Little League baseball to teach business owners in a manner they can relate to, in a writing style that keeps you wanting to turn the page. This isn't your typical book by a consultant with no real-world experience. It is clear that Earl has spent considerable time inside real businesses—actually leading them. I am going to give this book as a gift to all of my clients."

— Chad Blevins, President, Blevins Financial
www.BlevinsFinancial.com

A ROAD MAP TO SUCCESS FOR ENTREPRENEURS

WINNING in BASEBALL and BUSINESS

Transforming Little League Principles Into Major League Profits For Your Company

AVIVA
PUBLISHING
New York

EARL BELL

Winning in Baseball and Business: Transforming Little League Principles Into Major League Profits For Your Company

© 2012 by Earl Bell

ISBN: 978-1-938686-24-5
Library of Congress Control Number: 2012919897

Cover and Interior Book Design: Fusion Creative Works, www.fusioncw.com

Published By Aviva Publishing
Lake Placid, NY
518-523-1320
www.avivapubs.com

New York

www.WinninginBaseballandBusiness.com

$24.95 per copy + 9.5 percent sales tax for orders in Washington State.

To order this title by mail, please include price as noted above, $5.10 shipping for each book ordered. Send request to:

Earl Bell
8441 SE 68th Street, PMB #355
Mercer Island, WA 98040

Dedication

This book is dedicated to:

The true hero of our economy, the small business owner.

*My amazing wife Carrie with whom I recently
celebrated twenty years of marriage.*

*Lastly, my children, Alex, Carl, and Cara, who were wonderful
athletes and terrific teammates on the twenty-eight youth sports
teams I have coached since 2002. You were along for the
ride throughout this journey, and I've appreciated
you each and every day.*

Acknowledgments

This book could never have been written without inspiration provided by the 300-plus young athletes I've been fortunate enough to coach over the past ten years.

The top half of the 3rd inning chapter on culture in youth baseball was inspired by all the team moms who instantly "got it" and helped create a wonderful team experience each season. Special thanks to Shawn Taylor, Katerie Plummer, Vicki Pallis, Anne Emanuels and Merideth Tall—you all are ROCK STARS!

Mark Walters is a friend, business strategist, attorney, and trusted advisor to many—myself included. His thoughtful feedback and encouragement were invaluable! www.generalcounseltogo.com

Patrick Snow is, in my opinion, the world's best publishing coach—who possesses both a fountain of knowledge and an ocean of inspiration. www.patricksnow.com

Contents

INTRODUCTION

Realizing Your Dreams Through Business Ownership

Millions of business owners today are the struggling heroes of our economy, and their number is only increasing. Many of them are overworked, highly stressed, and barely making it.

If this description sounds like you, chances are the company you believed could one day be sold to fund your retirement and provide financial peace of mind is no longer able to provide this security. Not by a longshot! Let me ask a few questions: Do you question your vision, conviction, and fortitude to keep the company operating? Do you find that your passion is waning and your lifelong dreams are diminished if not extinguished? Is your business wearing you down?

If you answered "Yes" to any of these questions, I understand your pain and have been in your shoes. Having said that, I know a proven path that can take you from your current condition to realizing your personal goals through business ownership.

Winning in Baseball and Business shares many lessons I've learned over the years—both good and bad. Lessons learned on the Little League ball field are extremely transferable to the business world and boardroom, and vice-versa. The baseball experience and perspective shared in this book comes from serving as a board member and coach for select and Little League baseball and softball programs and teams over a ten-year period. The business experience and perspective comes from serving as a top level executive for over eighteen years with five different multi-million dollar companies that improved their annual profitability in seventeen of those years and created over $230 million in shareholder wealth. Also worth mentioning is that as these companies became increasingly more profitable, the effort it took to produce more profits actually decreased.

Over the years, I've experienced firsthand what works and what does not, and how to build value in organizations and conversely how to destroy it. I am passionate about helping individuals realize their dreams through business ownership—that is why I wrote this book.

Winning in Baseball and Business was written so you can learn exactly how to build a dramatically more valuable company while substantially increasing your income—by design and not chance. This book is logically sequenced to help guide your journey of creating a thriving company that produces sustainably increasing revenue and profits. An even more important desired outcome is for you to obtain greater amounts of discretionary time for other pursuits in life! This book is structured over "9 innings," or chapters, with the "10th extra inning" providing the secret formula for supercharging results.

In these pages, you are going to learn how to build a very successful and profitable company, which occurs in four logically sequenced stages.

The first stage and early innings are all about building a strong foundation for your company to grow—which begins in the 1st inning by clearly *Defining Success*. Without this clear definition of a desired destination, how can you know if you are moving your company in the right direction? *Answering "Why?"* is covered during the 2nd inning and is the foundational step that ensures your company will not be positioned as a commodity provider that becomes relegated to competing based on price while struggling to survive. The 3rd inning speaks to the importance of *Forming Strong Culture and Values*, the most critical thing you can do to build a sustainable foundation for realizing your personal and professional dreams through business ownership.

The second stage for building a highly profitable company is found in the middle innings of this book, which are about developing leaders, teams, strategies, tactics, execution, accountability, and alignment. During the 4th inning, *Assembling Leaders and Teams*, you will learn that strong leaders inspire followership in pursuit of a mission and vision along with ten attributes of effective leadership. You will also learn why it is important to send a strong message that teamwork matters. The 5th inning offers a basic framework for *Developing Strategy and Tactically Executing the Plan*. The 6th inning provides insight into how companies accelerate achievement of their goals by *Creating Alignment* throughout the entire company.

The third stage for achieving success through your business is found in the late innings of this book, which are about playing to win consistently. During the 7th inning, you will learn about *Investing In and Protecting Your Assets*. I'll ask you, "Do you know what your most important assets are, and if so, what are you doing to protect them, if anything?" The 8th inning is all about *Dealing With Risk*, exploring the five ways owners should think about, categorize, and manage business risk. In the 9th inning, you will learn why it is important to *Systematize Process* and I will give you a basic framework for thinking about how to transform business uncertainty into sustainable predictability.

The fourth and final stage, the 10th inning, will send your company on the path to hall of fame results by teaching you how to think about building a revenue-generating machine by *Building Advocacy and Relationships.*

Successfully completing each inning will improve the probability of an improved business outcome. Implementing work covered in additional innings will produce compounding benefits. Executing all steps will likely result in a transformation in your company and your personal outcomes.

The first half of each inning is dedicated to my personal journey coaching youth baseball. Included at the end of the each inning's first half is an inspirational story of a teen entrepreneur who has achieved success by employing the principle discussed. The second half is dedicated to business application of my personal experience and the baseball metaphors. Included at the end of each inning's second half is an inspirational story of a billionaire business person who has achieved success by the principle discussed. To get the maximum benefit from this book, be sure to complete the practice exercises found at the end of each inning, which are designed to help you develop a game plan to prepare you and your company for profitable business growth. I suggest you also keep a "game plan journal" for writing down any ideas you have for improving your business as you read. Reading this book should be fun and easy, but doing the work I suggest is difficult. However, if implemented, the financial and personal rewards will be well worth it.... My takeaway goal for you is that you learn how to *Apply Little League Principles to Achieve Major League Profits for Your Company.*

The time, effort, and money it takes to increase value dramatically in a company must be viewed as an investment and not an expense. For example, if you could invest $100,000 and get upwards of $1,000,000 in return, how many times would you make that investment? I'm guessing the answer is "every time."

The cover photo shows home plate on a ball field. Hitters literally have to step up to the plate when it is their turn at bat. A business owner has to do the same thing metaphorically while being bold—leading his or her company to greatness.

I want to serve as your coach, your mentor, and your accountability partner, so let's make this journey together. Following the business section of each inning is a series of exercises designed to stimulate thinking and get you closer to realizing your goals and dreams. If you want to receive maximum value, take the time to do each exercise. Practice by opening your mind and exploring what *could be*—then you will be well on your way to transforming potential into results. Are you ready to get started? Okay then—let's play ball....

PART I

The Early Innings

Foundational Work

1st INNING
Defining Success—Baseball

A MISSION STATEMENT....

One day, while standing in the Cooperstown National Baseball Hall of Fame with his son and grandson, a grandfather exclaimed... "Every kid in America should have the opportunity to play baseball in Cooperstown!"
— Lou Presutti Sr., who inspired his grandson to
build Cooperstown Dreams Park

Cooperstown, New York is home to the National Baseball Hall of Fame. Near the hall of fame is Doubleday Field, named after Abner Doubleday, who is credited with being the founder of baseball. This near-mythical place is where, each year, baseball players like Babe Ruth, Ty Cobb, and Lou Gehrig come to be honored as inductees into the hall of fame and also play ball during the induction week.

A MISSION REALIZED

In 1996, the vision of Lou Presutti Sr. would be realized by his grandson, Lou Presutti Jr. when Cooperstown Dreams Park, a baseball park designed for youth baseball tournaments, opened for business.

How cool is it to play baseball in Cooperstown, New York, to visit the National Baseball Hall of Fame, and to run the same bases on the field once shared by the greatest baseball players of all time? My twin boys and I would one day find out! Thirteen years after the opening of Cooperstown Dreams Park, I saw firsthand how Lou Presutti Jr.'s mission has positively impacted thousands of lives each summer.

The *baseball* half of this book chronicles the journey of building a youth baseball program on Mercer Island, Washington, which ultimately led to eleven boys, two coaches, and several families taking a magical trip to this remarkable baseball park during the week of August 15, 2009.

THE BEGINNING

My journey being involved in youth baseball began in March, 2003, when my wife, three children, in-laws, and I visited the Seattle Mariners spring training facility in Peoria, Arizona. Howard Lincoln, CEO of the Seattle Mariners and a family friend, was kind enough to take time out of his day to bring us onto one of the training ball fields where Mariner greats Ben Davis and John Olerud were taking hitting practice. From afar, these professional athletes already looked pretty big. In person and looking up from the eyes of a couple of six-year-old boys, they must have looked like superheroes!

While waiting for his turn at bat, Ben Davis bent down on one knee and started talking to my sons, Alex and Carl. They were mesmerized. In about thirty seconds, Ben shared the secrets of being a great hitter. He humbly mentioned what it took to be the best in the game and someday be recognized as a hall of fame player in Cooperstown. My boys took to heart every word—especially when Ben said, "When the pitcher releases the ball, you should close your eyes and swing with all your might," adding, "Seriously, this works—I do it all the time!" He winked and smiled at me, which the boys didn't quite catch. Nonetheless, a dream to play baseball was born within my sons and we were on our way! In April, 2003, Alex and Carl were signed up to play T-ball with the Mercer Island Boys & Girls Club.

One thing I've learned over time is that passion and clarity of mission are two initial elements that must be present to commence a long and meaningful journey. At the age of six, Alex and Carl had both an inspired passion and a clarity about their mission.

Their passion inspired me to become involved in building a youth select baseball program in my home community, which, ultimately, led to taking a baseball team to Cooperstown.

Whether we are talking about youth baseball or running a company, a meaningful journey starts with individuals who possess extreme passion and vision for their goals and dreams. What is your passion and vision for realizing your dreams through business ownership? Tap into *your* emotional triggers and get excited for your future!

DEFINITION OF SUCCESS

The definition of success starts with a mission statement, or in other words, the desired outcomes. So what does a mission statement look like for a successful youth baseball program?

In my opinion, such a statement includes a clause that reads, "*We will operate in a culture that puts kids first.*" One group that succeeds in creating such a culture is the Positive Coaching Alliance (PCA), a non-profit organization dedicated to developing winners in sports and life. The PCA views the playing field as the ideal place to teach life lessons. It notes that, too often, this ideal is sacrificed by the pursuit of winning at all costs, and it warns of the damage such a culture and environment can have on a program, teams, and players. In business, I suggest that a desirable clause in your mission statement should include, "*embracing a culture of putting your customers and clients first!*"

One of the best youth sports coaches I've ever met defined team success by stating, "If 90 percent of my players show up to play the following season, then I was a successful coach in the current season." By staying in the program each season, the players would become a "super team" in later years by elevating their skills, and more importantly, gelling as a cohesive team. It is true poetry-in-motion to watch the coach and his players when this cohesion occurs. A by-product of this philosophy for this coach and his team was two state championship teams, with the first championship team having 100 percent of its players stay through the program all four years.

This coach created an environment where the players would do anything and everything he asked because he inspired followership; in other words, he was and is a great leader. Being on his team was cool. The players understood that hard work and dedication could be fun; they were with their friends, and they developed a high level of competency at their position level and camaraderie and cohesion at the team level.

Looking inward at your business, does your company operate in an environment that truly enjoys serving customers? Do your good employees stay because they cannot imagine working anywhere else? Have you ever calculated the cost of employee turnover, especially when you lose "good employees" who were very valuable and important to your company's success? What would happen to the value of your company if your great employees never left and a "super team" were developed over the years?

Think about how your business can follow the model of the coach who defined success by retaining his players. Defining success in terms of putting kids first, developing winners in sports and life, is a superb model for creating a youth sports program mission statement. But exchange a few words (like *customer* for *kids, business* for *sports,* etc.) and you also have the makings of a great mission statement for your business.

A *DEFINITION OF SUCCESS mission statement* for a youth baseball program might look like this:

To build a strong and thriving program whose culture puts kids first where a measure of success is having 95 percent of all players sign up to play the following year. This will be accomplished by providing a venue where kids have fun playing with their friends, while developing baseball skills and life lessons that come from competing in a team sport environment. Coaches are provided adequate training and resources—and are selected based on their ability to serve kids in this capacity. Board members serve with the singular intent of ensuring that this mission statement is realized.

Little League Profile – Robert Nay

For some, the definition of success comes by achieving a goal set from a personal challenge.

At the age of fourteen, Robert Nay became a successful app developer. His first game, *Bubble Ball*, was downloaded more than two million times within two weeks of its launch. To put these numbers in perspective, the average mobile game receives a total of a few hundred downloads. *Bubble Ball* was so successful that it knocked the monster hit *Angry Birds* out of the number one most downloaded free game in the Apple app store.

The idea for *Bubble Ball* came from Robert's friends, who suggested he try making an iPhone app. He responded by saying, "That would be really cool" and moved forward with a specific mission to turn his vision into reality. With zero coding experience, Robert went to the public library to research how to create a game app.

In approximately one month, after doing some research and writing over 4,000 individual lines of code, *Bubble Ball* was complete. The total cost to produce the app was a nominal $1,200, which was given to Robert by his parents to purchase a new MacBook and necessary software licenses.

Currently available on both Apple and Android devices, *Bubble Ball* has been downloaded more than sixteen million times and counting. Robert started a mobile game development company called Nay Games and is working on developing "some awesome new stuff for *Bubble Ball* along with other gaming projects."

While Robert's fortune may yet lie in the future, he is getting his future customers engaged, having already found 16 million fans with Nay Games. How will he turn this attention into revenue? There are many possibilities, including selling future upgrades to his games ($1 per user is $16 million if everyone buys the upgrade), sell time/energy for game playtime, sell ad space, or sell his company outright to a strategic buyer. His possibilities for success are endless.

Robert's advice to other entrepreneurs is, "You can do amazing things if you just try."

Defining Success—Business

WHAT IS YOUR COMPANY'S MISSION STATEMENT?

The key to your future is clarity of mission. A mission statement defines why your business exists. Without a clearly defined mission statement, how can you expect to lead the company and employees toward creating an enterprise that realizes its potential as you've envisioned it to be? If you're going to design the preferred future with forward-looking intent, then you have to define and describe desired outcomes. My question is: "How simple yet descriptive can you be in your definition of success?"

Below is an example of a mission statement:

"To help entrepreneurs realize their dreams through business ownership."

This happens to be the mission statement for my business.

Regardless of what your company's mission statement is, getting your stakeholders aligned and supporting the mission statement will help big time in moving the company toward its aspirational goal and your goals! Start talking with your team about how to achieve the mission statement—there's no time like the present. By the way, this mission statement can also become your unique value proposition—the reason customers and clients would choose to do business with you.

So if the present is "now" and your aspirational goal is for "the future," how will you get there? Now isn't that an interesting puzzle to solve?

In later chapters, I'll talk about how to get there by using words like leadership, alignment of interests, improving probability of positive outcome, and reduction of business risk to develop a framework for dramatically building a more valuable company. However, it all starts with defining success.

First, it is time to write in your game plan journal what you have learned in this inning and how you can apply it to your business to improve your game. Take some time to answer the following questions as part of your company mission setting exercises:

What is your current mission statement as written?

_____

_____

_____

_____

_____

_____

What is your current company mission as you think about it? Does it answer the question "Why does your business exist?"

_____

_____

_____

_____

_____

_____

How does your company's current written mission statement align with how you currently think about the mission?

_____

_____

_____

_____

_____

This exercise calibrates how the company mission may have changed over time.

Was the mission statement built collaboratively from the bottom up in the company or imposed from the top down?

_____

_____

_____

_____

_____

_____

_____

_____

_____

_____

The second question's answer speaks to your leadership style, which we will talk about during the 4th inning.

Is there organizational alignment with the company's mission, meaning does everyone in the company understand its reason for being in business and its aspirational goal?

The third question's answer focuses on the issue of organizational alignment, which we will talk about during the 6th inning.

WHAT IS THE PERSONAL VISION FOR YOUR BUSINESS?

While owning a business carries a certain amount of risk, the potential rewards are limited only by the limits of your vision, or by your ability to execute on that vision. While understanding that only you limit yourself is a profound thing to think about, it is absolutely true in every sense of the word.

So, have you thought about some tangible outcomes that could become your personal vision and success statement as it relates to the business? Below are some examples:

I want to grow my company's revenue from ____ to ____.

I want to increase profitability and cash from __ to __.

I want to have less day-to-day involvement in the business because discretionary time is the purest definition of wealth.

I want to retire in ____ years.

I want to sell my company in ____ years.

Every one of these personal vision and success statements could apply to you. Then again, you may have very different ideas about what you want from your company. Think through the level of alignment between the company mission statement, your personal vision, and the outcomes statement.

Continue writing in your game plan journal and answer the following questions as part of your personal vision setting exercise:

What are your personal vision statement and desired outcomes from business ownership?

How many years are you willing to invest to achieve your vision?

_____

_____

_____

If you were to sell your company, how much money do you need to receive on a net basis in order to fund your retirement goals? This number is calculated by starting with your sales proceeds, which is then reduced by all transaction expenses including income taxes.

_____

_____

_____

How will you know whether your vision was achieved?

_____

_____

_____

_____

_____

_____

_____

Having completed these vision exercises to help define success, take additional time to write down these goals on a single sheet of paper—in bullet point form. Laminate the sheet and look at it every day.

To wrap up this inning, be clear about setting your vision and defining success—then getting there will be easier.

Obstacles are those frightful things you see when you take your eyes off your goal.
— Henry Ford

SCORING THE GAME:

If you can clearly define success in a succinct mission statement where *everyone* in the organization embraces the mission, you will be able to compete in the game of business. Bonus base runners are awarded if you can clearly define the personal goals and vision for success through your business.

If your company's mission or vision is unclear—to yourself and those charged with helping you execute on reaching this blurry mission and/or vision—well…I'd recommend that you start thinking about finding a new game to play….

1st INNING SCORECARD

What are your key takeaways from this first inning?

_____

_____

_____

_____

_____

_____

_____

_____

_____

_____

_____

_____

_____

_____

_____

_____

_____

_____

_____

Major League Profile – Ray Kroc

Ray Kroc's definition of success was not to make the best hamburger in the world, but to make the most consistent hamburger in the world.

Kroc is the man who turned McDonald's into a fast food empire that has served billions of hamburgers and whose restaurants can be found all over the world. While visiting the McDonalds brothers' hamburger restaurant, he watched burger after burger being churned out like clockwork. He eventually bought the business for $2.7 million and then changed the fast-food dining industry forever by creating an assembly line method of selling burgers that became the worldwide standard and a multi-billion dollar business.

Kroc offered two leadership lessons:

1. **Have a big vision:** Leaders have vision and when viewing a certain situation, they see the potential and not the present. They have an ability to visualize the future and what it takes to realize this dream. As a leader, you too must always try to think about the possibilities.

2. **Be committed to excellence:** As a leader, you must be committed to every single detail in your plans. Your commitment to details becomes your commitment to excellence, and this commitment will differentiate you from your competitors. By setting and holding yourself to this high standard, your followers will be inspired to do the same.

2nd INNING

Answering "Why?"—Baseball

WHAT'S IN IT FOR THE PLAYERS?

To have a successful youth baseball program, enough players are needed to form a league; similarly, a business must have enough customers to sustain it. To obtain those customers, begin by seeking to understand the answer to this question with 100 percent clarity: "*Why* do kids sign up to play?"

Based on my experience and post-season feedback received over a five-year period, the two main reasons kids sign up to play Little League and select youth baseball are: 1) having fun, and 2) playing with their friends. For select baseball players, there is also a desire to play against high level competition.

If a program fails to deliver on these goals, chances are low for building a league that sustains itself year-after-year.

Looking at youth baseball from a boy's perspective, the benefits are:

1. To play a fun game (after all, it is a game).

2. To hang out with his friends.

3. To learn new skills while becoming part of a team.

4. To learn how to compete.

Now, instead of thinking about youth baseball from a ten-year-old boy's perspective, start thinking about your company and customers. Is there a compelling reason why customers buy from your company? Does your business deliver a "must have" product, service, or customer experience? Or is it providing more of a commodity that customers can pretty much get anywhere? Are there competitors who are taking market share from you because they do a better job of answering, "Why should customers buy from me?"

Great value takes many shapes and forms. Tangible value is the "dollars and sense" behind a transaction. For example, is the player getting $200 value from playing Little League baseball? The left side or logical side of the brain is forming this decision. Chances are, tangible value means very little to the player.

Great intangible experience is "how the season went." It describes how a player feels after each practice, game, and season's end. Did the coach create a fun team? Did the player learn new skills? Did he enjoy playing as part of this team? Does he want to do this again? Both tangible value and intangible experience play into the ultimate question "Will the player sign up to play baseball again next year?" I'll bet that the intangible and emotional experience is the more important! In other words, the right side of the brain is dominant in calculating value received by the player. Don't underestimate the value of this insight in relation to the world of business!

Predictable outcome is the third critical element of a successful youth baseball program. You want a good experience—every year. Imagine what happens if a player has a great season for four years in a row, but the fifth season, he has a megalomaniac for a coach and a horrible season. Chances are this player will be looking for a new sport next year. If this situation happens with enough regularity, players will migrate en masse from one sport to another. When this happens "The tribe has spoken!" Imagine if this migration happened within your business!

WHAT'S IN IT FOR THE PARENTS?

So, why does a parent sign up a son or daughter to play youth baseball, and why does he or she serve as a board member of the program or volunteer as a coach? Over the years, I've discovered the reasons are in the dozens, which in part makes the process of creating a thriving program challenging.

Many volunteer board members and coaches simply want to give back to their communities so they see these roles as their opportunities to serve. They have no hidden agendas. Several other board members want to secure preferential treatment for their kids in the program or for themselves as coaches in the program. What makes youth baseball so challenging to manage with an eye toward the future is wildly shifting motivations among the constantly rotating leadership at the board and coaching level. The same problems can happen in the business world.

Many team parents want to provide their sons and daughters an opportunity to play "America's Pastime." They are great supporters, fans, and champions of the game. Several other parents place unbearable pressure on their kids to perform, as if their son or daughter's performance somehow will reflect on them personally, whether in a positive or negative way.

It is this very lack of clarity and alignment of interests that makes running a youth baseball program difficult to sustain year-after-year. Increasing alignment with respect to answering the question "Why?" increases the probability of delivering a high quality youth baseball experience. The Little League program in which I am currently involved is doing many good things to move in this direction. So can *your* business—read on!

If the answer to "Why?" is as varied as shades on the color spectrum, so will be results delivered to those being served. To build a strong youth baseball program, be singularly focused on why the program exists, who it serves (players), and how it serves (creating an awesome experience that has the player telling his friends how much fun he is having!)

Little League Profile – Lizzie Marie Likness

Helping others to live a healthy lifestyle is a terrific reason why this entrepreneur's business matters. An aspiring chef since age two, now at eleven years old, Lizzie Marie Likness is living her *why* and well on her way to becoming the next generation's Rachael Ray.

At age six, Lizzie yearned to take horseback riding lessons. She wanted them so badly that she offered to help pay for the lessons. When asked by her parents where she would get the money, she said, "I'll sell healthy homemade baked goods at the local farmer's market."

This idea resulted in Lizzie becoming the founder of Lizzie Marie Cuisine, which she says is unique because, "I teach kids how to have fun cooking healthy meals and how to live healthy."

Within a few years, word got around regarding her original recipes and ability to empower young people. Invitations came in to demonstrate her cooking prowess with celebrity chefs at major live events, such as Taste of Atlanta.

Lizzie was asked to become a spokesperson for the American Heart Association's "Go Red for Women" campaign, and the Atlanta Falcons' "First Down For Fitness Program." In 2011, she also appeared as a guest on *The Rachael Ray Show*.

Currently, Lizzie is the star of the WebMD Fit Channel's series *Healthy Cooking with Lizzie*. She recently signed a branded entertainment and

TV development deal with the New York based production company, DBG, and global digital marketing agency, Digitas.

This young entrepreneur who lives in Georgia expects the future to include launching a series of healthy cooking cookbooks, packaged food products, and new digital media shows.

She offers the following advice for budding entrepreneurs: "The greatest reward is doing what you love for the good of others."

ANSWERING "WHY?"—BUSINESS

In the 1st inning, I asked you to define success by developing a mission and vision statement.

So, are you comfortable with what your mission and vision statements say and represent? If "Yes," let's keep going. If "No," invest the time and come up with a clear mission and vision before continuing. This type of journey takes time—and we want to get it right!

Okay. Now that you've brought clarity to the definition of success, let's move on to the concept of defining why customers should buy from your company.

WHAT'S IN IT FOR THE CUSTOMER?

The first thing to understand 100 percent, if you're going to be successful in business, is: "*Why* do people buy my products or services?" If you don't understand the emotional and logical reasons why your customers buy from you, and the unique value you provide, how can you expect them to? Throughout this book, I talk repeatedly about how to solve the puzzle of creating very valuable companies. And it all starts with being clear about why customers do business with you.

I'm sure you've heard the maxim that buyers purchase based on emotion and support their decisions based on logic. With this being the case, if your customers cannot understand on an emotional level *why* they should buy your product or service *and* understand the great value they receive from your product or service, chances are they won't do so on a repeated basis, so you'll be leaving lots of value on the table. Get this right if you want to build an extremely successful organization! Get this wrong and you will become a commodity business that competes strictly based on price—a guaranteed way to lower your profits, cash flow, and viability as a healthy company.

While a variety of businesses exist that provide countless products and services, all out-performing companies share an ability to excel at a few simple things. Let's use one type of business to illustrate my point.

Think about your favorite restaurant. It's a place that makes you feel welcome, puts a smile on your face, and leaves you excited to return. Chances are you are receiving:

1. Great tangible value.

2. A great intangible experience.

3. A predictable and consistent outcome.

Great value takes many shapes and forms. Tangible value is the dollars and sense behind the business transaction. Could you have created the same meal at home for less money? If not, was the time saved by not having to shop for ingredients, cook the meal, and clean up afterwards part of your value received? The left side, or logical side of the brain, drives this calculation of value.

Great intangible experience is the overall ambiance created by the restaurant's owner, management, and staff. Did the greeter create a positive first impression? Were you seated at a good table? If you are a repeat customer, do the servers know you by name? Do they make you feel welcome and glad to be their guest? Do you see friends at the restaurant bar over a glass of wine before sitting down for dinner?

Both tangible value and intangible experience are important reasons why you choose your favorite restaurant. But I'll bet that the intangible experience is more valuable to you! In other words, the right side of the brain is dominant in calculating value received. Studies show that people go out to eat for the experience, not the food. Don't underestimate the value of this insight!

Predictable outcome is the third critical element of a successful restaurant. You want the same experience—every time. McDonald's is a successful franchise not because it consistently makes the best hamburgers in the world, but because you know exactly what you are getting, regardless of which McDonald's you visit. Imagine going to your favorite restaurant, and eight times out of ten, the experience is amazing. However, two out of ten visits are simply awful—with overcooked food coupled with slow and rude service. Chances are you will be looking for a new favorite restaurant. A success ratio of 80 percent would guarantee championship status on any sports team, but probably relegates a service business into the "also ran" category—or perhaps a page in the long history book of failed restaurants.

COMPELLING BUSINESS PURPOSE

To make sure you really understand what I'm trying to say, let me give you another way to think about why a compelling business purpose is important. What would be the impact to your customers if your company no longer existed? Many business owners and executives are taken aback when I ask that question, but I ask it for good reason. After I ask the question a second time, a blank stare is usually followed by "I don't know how to answer that."

So, think about it. What would happen if your company were no longer in business? Would customers and clients shrug and then move along to do business with one of your competitors? Would their lives be negatively impacted as a result of your company or firm no longer serving them? If your answer is "No," I'll respond by saying that your business does not add *significant* value that is distinguishable from competitors! I'm also guessing that the income you draw from your business is not as high as you'd like it to be, your company is not worth as much as you'd like, and you're working more hours than you ever envisioned.

51

To be truly successful in business, I believe one of the first things you have to develop with absolute clarity is the compelling purpose or reason why customers purchase your product or clients use your services. Another way to think about this same question is to ask, "Why would someone buy from me instead of someone else? What makes my company unique and remarkable, so much so that a customer cannot imagine doing business with someone who could be considered my competitor?"

Invest the time to figure this out. Make your company unique and remarkable so customers can't go elsewhere. Then you'll be on your way to building value in your company—by delivering great value to your customers and clients.

If applicable, are you willing to raise your hand and say, "I don't have a compelling business purpose?" If so, what will you do about it and when will you do it? If you do nothing, what will be the cost of doing nothing about it?

THE POWER OF AUTHENTIC BUSINESS LANGUAGE

Language is powerful but often misunderstood. In fact, what you say is not what others necessarily hear and repeat to others. Understanding this potential confusion and bringing clarity to authentic business language is key to attracting perfect customers and clients.

Lucas Mack, principal and founder of 4th Avenue Media, posits that "If a language defines a culture and every business has a culture, then every business must have a language."

To capitalize on this epiphany, Lucas has created a proprietary and specialized test that captures your unique business language and culture, which in turn drives your internal brand integrity. This process is called a "mirror test."

My first question to you is: What is the language of your business? I'm guessing you don't know exactly what I'm talking about, and quite frankly, there is a significant downside to not understanding, articulating, and building clarity and alignment around your unique business language. The downside is that you sound like everyone else—and are viewed as a commodity.

My second question is: What is the cost to your company of not understanding the language of your business? How many potential customers are lost because your business language is unclear? How many customers are you attracting who really aren't a good fit, but neither you nor the customer is aware of it? Dramatically increasing value in your company is a lot easier when you bring clarity and alignment to the way you communicate with others.

I've recently invested in the "mirror test." The outcome of my investment was realizing, with 100 percent clarity, my business' language. The results were eye-opening and will help me attract perfect customers! A reader on my website reached out, and after a quick discussion, became a client, because I used authentic business language to describe my compelling business purpose. In fact, I've already received a 300 percent return on my investment—I was astonished since it's only been one month. My coaching and consulting practice exists to help owners realize their dreams through entrepreneurship. Primary outcomes clients receive by working with me are dramatic increases in three areas: their companies' value, their personal income, and discretionary time to pursue life's interests outside of their businesses.

Based on results from my mirror test, 4th Avenue Media produced eight video clips that are now on my website at www.islandcrestconsulting.com. They are located throughout the website, but currently can be found on the Homepage, the About-Why Earl page and under the Resources tab. Lucas suggested that the video clips will provide greater clarity regarding the language of my business. My charge to you is: Embrace the power of authentic business language and your unique brand integrity!

The concepts laid out in this section are critical to understand; they lay the foundation for everything else we will talk about in this book. Before continuing further, I encourage you to take a few minutes to write some notes down in your game plan journal and to articulate clearly the answers to the following questions:

What are the tangible reasons for why customers buy from my company? What is the value they receive from these tangible reasons?

_____

_____

_____

_____

_____

_____

_____

_____

_____

_____

_____

_____

_____

_____

_____

_____

_____

_____

_____

_____

_____

_____

What are the intangible reasons why customers buy from my company? What is the value they receive from these intangibles?

_____

_____

_____

_____

_____

_____

_____

_____

_____

_____

_____

_____

_____

_____

_____

_____

_____

_____

_____

_____

_____

_____

What are the reasons why potential customers DO NOT buy from my company?

_____

_____

_____

_____

_____

_____

_____

_____

_____

_____

_____

_____

_____

_____

_____

_____

_____

Do I deliver great value and a consistent experience to encourage loyalty and repeat business?

If so, what am I doing right? If not, what needs to change?

_____

_____

_____

_____

_____

_____

_____

_____

_____

_____

_____

_____

_____

_____

_____

_____

_____

_____

Is the language of my business powerful, authentic, and unique?

If not, what does it cost me annually in lost revenue and profits by *not* providing clarity to potential customers?

If not, what needs to change?

In the world of youth baseball and the ten-year-old boy, possible answers may look something like this:

1. **Tangible reasons I signed up for Little League baseball this year:** To become a better baseball player and be part of a team. I got this experience last year and want to do it again!

2. **Intangible reasons I signed up for Little League baseball this year:** To have fun and play with my friends. I got this experience last year and want to do it again!

3. **Reasons I DID NOT play Little League baseball this year:** The coaches suck and play favorites. They yell and scream and make the game miserable. It is NOT fun and the experience was awful last year.

4. **Was the Little League experience consistent?** Not at all. Some coaches are good and others stink. Some teams had all the good players and destroyed their opponents every time. I am going to play another sport this year.

If the goal is to build a sustainable and growing youth baseball program, the league would be well-served to deliver what the players want and build a culture where coaches serve the players. In business, achieving this goal means focusing on the customer first!

WHAT'S IN IT FOR THE BUSINESS OWNER?— PERSONAL GOALS

So *why* did you become a business owner? If the answer is "I don't know exactly," then it is time to tap into the emotional reasons that will ultimately drive your success. Without explicitly understanding the *why*, chances are you are simply going through the motions of business ownership, and if that is the case, you could be leaving millions of dollars of value on the table (your financial future).

To help you figure out your why, let's begin by exploring the personal outcomes business owners typically desire through ownership in their companies.

Many business owners began their entrepreneurial pursuits by purchasing or starting a very small enterprise, desiring to build a company that could someday be sold for a substantial amount of money and would provide a healthy retirement fund. Does this sound like you? How much is your company worth today? How much more valuable does your company need to be for you to retire with the lifestyle you desire? How will you get there? Do you know how to build value in your company or the steps that work every time? If not, don't worry—that's why you purchased this book!

Many business owners also start their companies after leaving the corporate world with the idea that "I'll never have a boss again." The company is built around the owner in such a way that all major decisions are made by the owner. Usually, this owner works sixty-plus hours per week to keep the company afloat. Does this sound like you? Have you fallen into the "lifestyle business owner trap" and do not know how to get out of it? Do you understand the value of more discretionary time? Is getting greater work/life balance a distant dream for you? If so, be patient and keep reading; you'll receive lots of valuable information and thoughts to help you on this journey.

Yet another group of owners desire to build and leave a legacy. These owners are proud of the companies they built and want nothing more than to pass along the business to family members. Unfortunately, most of the time, the next generation isn't ready to assume ownership and leadership responsibilities. At the same time, the owner isn't emotionally ready to cede control to the next generation owners. Call me Nostradamus, but this sounds like a recipe for disaster. Does this scenario seem all too familiar? Do you know what it takes to build a business of real lasting value that can survive without your participation? It's time to start thinking about this—before it is too late!

Okay. I've listed three possible personal reasons why people choose to become a business owner. What's more important is for you to understand clearly and articulate the personal reasons why you are a business owner. Dig deeply into these reasons and write them down on a sheet of paper that you can look at every day. I'll explain why later....

Before moving forward, continue writing in your game plan journal and answer this question:

Why am I a business owner—the personal reasons?

Be clear about what motivates you personally. It will help to keep you focused on future success.

In youth baseball programs, motivations for serving as a league coach or board member are varied. The most successful leagues are run by true servant leaders or parents who want to create a top-notch program and experience for all the kids, not just their sons, or even worse, their own egos.

WHAT'S IN IT FOR THE BUSINESS OWNER?— PROFESSIONAL GOALS

Being the CEO and owner has its share of responsibility and pressure. It also can and should be a very rewarding part of your life—if you focus on the desired outcomes by tapping into your professional goals for being the CEO/owner. I'll suggest that if you are miserable and lack passion at work, it might have something to do with the way you define the job and how it defines you. Starting with the end in mind, let's agree that professional goal #1 should be to have extremely high satisfaction and passion in your role as CEO. Professionally speaking, this satisfaction and passion should be the answer to the question "Why?"

Most business owners like to solve puzzles, personally and professionally. Part of the business puzzle to be solved might involve answering, "How do I build a sustainable company with collaborative teams that provides a product or service that is always in high demand—and in such a way that profitability and cash flow increases year after year, almost in a predictable way." If learning the answer to this question sounds interesting to you, then I would ask, "On a scale of 1 to 10, how far along are you in solving this puzzle in your business?" If you have a ways to go, which I imagine applies to most readers, what specifically do you need to work on? What's holding you back? How long will it take? What are the risks that can blow up your plan? If you were to solve these difficult business questions, would you have high satisfaction in your role as a CEO? I'm guessing the answer is "Absolutely!" I would hope that all business leaders want their companies to increase predictably their profits and cash flows.

Recently, I gave a keynote speech to a group of business owners. During a brief Question and Answer session, I asked, "What is the biggest professional outcome you desire as CEO?" A terrific answer was "To be able to continue hiring employees as my company grows." Now this was a business owner who saw his company as an instrument for providing a much-needed product for his customers that, in turn, produced more jobs resulting from his business being able to grow in a profitable way. In other words, his job as CEO wasn't about him so much as about serving others. Being able to hire others provided this business owner much professional satisfaction in his job.

Okay. I've listed three possible professional reasons why people choose to become business owners. What's more important is for you to understand and articulate the professional reasons *you* are a business owner. Write down these reasons on a sheet of paper you can look at every day. Those who look at written goals on a daily basis tend to focus more on achieving their goals.

Before moving forward, write in your game plan journal and answer this question:

Why am I a business owner—the professional reasons?

_____

_____

_____

_____

_____

_____

_____

_____

_____

_____

_____

_____

_____

_____

_____

_____

_____

_____

Be clear about what motivates you professionally. It will help keep you focused on future success.

The more people you inspire, the more people will inspire you.

— Simon Sinek, author of *Start With Why:*
How Great Leaders Inspire Everyone to Take Action

SCORING THE GAME:

If you can clearly articulate the tangible and intangible answers to *why* customers buy from you, and you can also define the great value they receive, you will be able to compete in the game of business. Bonus base runners are awarded if you can identify the reasons customers currently DO NOT buy from you, and you can make the mid-inning adjustments to turn negatives into positives.

If you cannot do so, it's time to relegate yourself to the group of "al-so-ran" companies that will ultimately compete on price alone and be perceived as one "commodity" provider that provides non-differentiated value, which is no different from anyone else. But don't get too comfortable settling there; the game will soon be over for you....

2nd INNING SCORECARD

What are your key takeaways from this 2nd inning?

_____

_____

_____

_____

_____

_____

_____

_____

_____

_____

_____

_____

_____

_____

_____

_____

_____

_____

Major League Profile – Steve Jobs

Steve Jobs founded Apple in the 1970s. He epitomizes *why* Apple is more innovative than any other computer company and *how* great leaders inspire action.

Jobs and the team at Apple truly believed in thinking differently. They always challenged the status quo. They made products that were user-friendly and elegantly designed, which kept customers always excited to try and buy Apple's new products.

The iPod transformed the way people listened to music. The iPhone transformed cell phone users into smart phone users. Customers believed in what Apple believed in as it continued always to challenge the status quo. Under Steve Jobs' leadership, Apple became the most valuable company in the world.

Jobs offered two leadership lessons:

1. **Persistence is the key to success:** As a leader, you must be ready to face setbacks. Whether or not you become successful often depends on your ability never to give up and its application to your leadership and your team's characteristics.

   Jobs was ousted from Apple Computer during the early years. He went on to start NeXT computers, which would eventually be acquired by Apple Computer. That year, he returned to become CEO of Apple Computer. Most people would have given up and spent years being bitter over their loss.

2. **Innovation attracts leadership:** Regardless of your industry, constantly innovate in alignment with your business mission—doing so will keep you ahead of the competition.

   To maintain leadership, Jobs was the one who constantly came up with new ideas and innovations in pursuit of the company's mission.

3rd INNING
Forming Culture and Values—Baseball

During the 1st inning, I suggested that defining success and developing a powerful mission statement for running a strong youth baseball program must include verbiage about *putting kids first while developing winners in sports and life*.

During the 2nd inning, I suggested that clearly understanding *why* kids sign up to play youth baseball, and delivering on that expectation, is what enables youth baseball programs and teams to be successful.

Well, let's assume for a minute that ALL youth baseball leagues have a powerful mission statement and understand the answer to *why*. If that were the case, a good rhetorical question to puzzle over would be "Why do some leagues have a thriving program with tons of kids who sign up to play year after year while other leagues struggle?" I'm guessing that those leagues that struggle haven't invested the time you are now taking to master the simple but profound concepts covered in this book, which by the way, will help you build a thriving company!

This all important 3rd inning is all about forming the culture and values that enable a league and teams to be successful. If culture and values aren't everything, they sure are darn close!

Culture and values is a fancy way of saying, "This is the way our league and teams operate." Imagine if your youth baseball program created an environment where every child athlete has a high-quality experience as a result of high quality coaching. What if…? Wouldn't that be awesome!

Examples of how this type of culture might look could include:

- Coaches are uniformly trained to serve the athletes by providing a fun environment in a positive culture.

- Coaches are supported by other coaches, parents, fans, umpires, and athletes—all of whom learn to compete while honoring the game and its rules.

- Every athlete has an important role to play on the team. Not everyone will be a star performer but all athletes can contribute to the team's success. Coaches take time to recognize successful team behavior. Each athlete feels valued as an important team member.

- Coaches and athletes learn life lessons from the game and their experience of a season.

- Athletes, parents, and fans have an awesome experience and tell all of their friends!

Now substitute the words *business leader* for *coach*, *employee* for *athlete*, *customer* for *parents*, and *vendor* for *fan*…. You get the idea. Such examples of positive culture in baseball also apply to business!

So the page above provided examples of what a positive culture looks like for a youth baseball program. Let's talk briefly about what a negative culture looks like, so you will be aware of what NOT to do—by turning the culture upside down where the league, team, and players are all designed to serve a select group of team coaches and players.

"What?" you say. "That's nuts!" Well, let's explore what this scenario might look like....

Have you ever seen a coach who seems intent on winning at all costs? Such coaches' behaviors might include yelling at umpires to try and sway decisions. As a result, parents and players think the umpire is cheating the team and they develop bad attitudes. Alternatively, have you seen a coach who lavishes praise on players who make good plays while berating those who make errors? These coaches often work behind the scenes to get a team stacked in their favor to feed their egos because winning a game is what really matters. Meanwhile, kids who aren't "stars" in these coaches' eyes become despondent and have a miserable experience. They complain to their friends, and eventually, the program begins to crumble because the CULTURE WAS NEGATIVE! I call this type of culture *The Vortex of Doom*.

I have many friends all over the country who tell stories very similar to my *Vortex of Doom* illustration. I imagine a lot of struggling companies look the same way, if you were to take the story above and replace the word *coach* with *business leader*. In other words, bad things happen when business leaders become arrogant and believe the company is designed to serve them and not the other way around.

So here is a bonus piece of advice: If you want to see what kind of a leader you are about to hire, find out if he coaches a youth sports team, and if he does, go check out his style of coaching in a game. You may learn a lot about him over the course of a two-hour game.

Little League Profile – Catherine, Dave, and Geoff Cook

In 2005, when Catherine Cook and her brother Dave were fifteen and seventeen years old, respectively, they decided to stay true to their company's founding mission, values, and culture, which enabled them to take their company on an amazing ride.

At the very beginning and while flipping through their high school yearbook, they came up with an idea to develop a free interactive online version. After convincing their older brother Geoff to invest his time and $250,000 to launch this business idea, the social-networking site MyYearbook.com was born.

After merging with Zenhex.com, an ad-supported site where users post various types of homemade quizzes, the number of viewers on their site quickly doubled. Potential investors wanted to move the company to New York and also have ads appear on users' personal profile pages, which the founders did not support.

Staying true to founding ideals proved to be the right move for the Cooks. The year after launching the business, MyYearbook raised $4.1 million from U.S. Venture Partners and First Round Capital. The profile of advertisers became increasingly higher, with Neutrogena, Disney, and ABC purchasing ad space. A series of additional right moves led to a pretty successful outcome. In July 2011, MyYearbook agreed to be acquired by Latino social networking site Quepasa for $100 million in cash and stock.

Forming Culture and Values–Business

The 3rd inning as it relates to business is all about articulating clearly a defined culture and values statement for your company that is supportive of your mission and vision statements. Why do some companies thrive while others struggle? Many of those that struggle haven't invested the time you are now taking to master the simple but profound concepts covered in the first three innings of this book.

By the way, *only* after successfully completing the first three innings of this book should you begin to think about things like leadership, team building, and developing a long-term strategy. To do otherwise is putting the cart before the horse.

Keep your definition of culture and values simple so it will always be easy for everyone inside and outside of the company to understand the *container* by which your company operates. If for some reason the company tilts away from defined culture and values, it will also be easier to recognize and adjust back to its guiding roots.

CULTURE EATS STRATEGY FOR LUNCH

To illustrate what I mean by *Culture Eats Strategy for Lunch*, I'd like to share two stories about two Seattle area companies that realized how company culture and values created the *container* that enabled explosive, sustainable, and profitable growth. While reading these examples, think of a box container as a metaphor for company culture and values. In other words, a cardboard box soaked in water—*the proverbial weak container*—will fall apart, regardless of the contents and value inside the container. This is a metaphor for saying that in business, the most brilliant strategy and tactical execution plans will usually fail if the organization's culture and values are weak or unaligned throughout. Conversely, a strong culture with aligned values throughout the company will significantly improve the probability of a successful execution of business strategy and tactical plans.

On CNBC, I recently watched a broadcast "The Costco Craze—Inside the Warehouse Giant" in which Jim Sinegal, Costco's recently retired CEO, acknowledged that the company culture wasn't the most important thing contributing to Costco's success and growth—it was the *only* thing!

In a nutshell, Costco's culture looks like this: Members and employees come first at Costco. Bringing a good value to the stores and providing members with great service is really what everyone does there. If an item does not provide a great deal for the customer, the item will not be carried in the stores. Employees are well-paid, work hard in a fun environment, and tend to stay with the company for long periods of time. Costco's culture is easy to understand and has proven to be a very strong yet simple container that works extremely well.

To cite another example, I had lunch earlier this year at the Capital Grille in downtown Seattle with Ron Elgin, who recently retired as Chairman and CEO of DDB Seattle, part of an international advertising agency. I asked Ron to name the #1 contributing factor that had enabled his company to grow in thirty years from a humble start-up to over $250 million in annualized billings.

He replied, "We started with the idea that company culture meant we wouldn't work with or for assholes!" Essentially, the "no asshole filter" worked something like this: After a prospective employee went through the technical aspects of the hiring process, Ron would meet with the candidate. If he felt the candidate fit within the specific culture of DDB Seattle, he was hired. If not, well…that's how the filtering process works!

Taking these two examples into consideration, think about what's most important to your company's growth and health. Do you have difficult employees who make life miserable in the workplace? Are you that person in your company? Is it difficult to execute on strategic goals because things like collaboration and accountability don't work when a person or team is toxic to the organization? The saying "Culture Eats Strategy" has been around for a while because it's true.

This is very important—get company culture right!

VALUES STATEMENT

The word *values* is another way to talk about company culture. I am fascinated by why some businesses succeed and others struggle to survive. I've noticed that great companies have a *widely known and accepted* "values statement" that provides *guiding principles* about a company's core beliefs and mission to serve its customers.

So why are shared values important? I'm here to tell you that it's all part of the alignment equation that great companies solve before becoming dominant in their niches.

Taking the Costco and DDB Seattle examples into consideration, let's pretend that the following are your company's guiding principles:

1. Develop long-lasting and meaningful relationships with our clients.

2. Always prioritize a client's best interests over our own.

3. Treat everyone with kindness and respect.

4. Maintain balance between work, family, and community.

Strong values and guiding principles provide the fabric for weaving a company culture. They offer rules of engagement regarding how employees treat each other, customers, vendors, and other stakeholders. The culture becomes who they are—inside and outside of the company.

So let's also pretend for a moment that you, as CEO of the company, have an opportunity to hire a new VP of Sales who previously has seemed to switch jobs every two or three years, but has always demonstrated tremendous sales growth at each job. By the way, this person's guiding principles look like this:

1. Revenue growth is good, regardless of circumstance.

2. Finding a way to close the deal is goal #1.

3. The top sales team gets the most commissions—sales departments support the company.

4. Work defines who I am.

To hire or not to hire this person? That is the hypothetical question. Which would you do?

If you would hire this person, despite the fact that your company's values are 180 degrees different from his, chances are your short-term revenue goals will be met, but:

1. Revenue will be transaction-driven (short-term in nature) instead of relationship-driven (long-term—almost like an annuity). The company will be serving customers who aren't a good long-term fit; all in the name of helping this salesperson achieve his quota.

2. Profitability will suffer, as margins decline when sales teams focus on price cutting to close deals and earn commissions instead of serving clients.

3. Work becomes all-consuming and employees burn out and leave, leading to turnover concerns.

If you did not hire this person, it's because you understand that maintaining corporate culture and identity is what enables your "work family" to be successful and helps you sustainably to build a more valuable company. I hope you did the latter....

THE CULTURE/VALUE OF PLANNING

Leadership needs to build a culture where proactively planning for the future is an important element in the formula for creating success. Most CEOs, based on research done at Fortune 1000 companies, use less than 8 percent of their time to plan for the future. These are very large companies with enormous resources, so the CEO shouldn't have to be constantly mired in the details. But for the small to mid-size company to compete successfully, I think it is a recipe for disaster when the leader isn't spending the time necessary to make sure the company is moving forward in pursuit of its vision and strategic goals. As a data point for benchmarking what successful executives do, Ron Elgin, the highly successful CEO I mentioned earlier, spent about 70 percent of his time proactively planning for the future. I believe that for the reader of this book, spending at least 20 percent of his or her time thinking about the future in a strategic manner is a good benchmark.

To illustrate by providing another example of inserting planning into company culture, below is an excerpt from a guest post on my business blog site written by Dave Shapiro, CEO of Excell Puget Sound, a CEO peer group program.

"Sales" was one of many places culture and values affected the firm [Dave's client]. Too little time was spent on it because the key partners did all the selling. They put their firm at risk by not allowing, let alone encouraging, their juniors to sell. Tracking only billable hours also meant that the two hours we had just spent were not valued by his partners (no credit given). I told this client that until he actually thought of what we did as work and got credit and acknowledgment from his partners, they would continue to bump into the ceiling they were at (the inability to grow revenue and number of professionals).

You could see the light bulb go on. My client thanked me and we worked another hour on planning how to begin shifting the culture at his firm so it could grow in a sustainably profitable way.

Let's review key takeaways before I give you a practice drill to work on.

Healthy culture is a valuable asset.

Strong culture and values provide the container that enables a company to thrive. Culture eats strategy for lunch—get it right!

Inversely speaking, toxic cultures will eventually destroy companies.

A company's values statement provides guiding principles about a company's core beliefs to fulfill its mission to serve its customers.

Okay. Now it is time to continue writing in your game plan journal and to answer the following questions to start developing or redefining your company culture:

If you could define the culture and values that would maximize your ability to build a thriving company, what would those attributes look like?

_____

_____

_____

_____

_____

_____

_____

_____

_____

_____

_____

_____

_____

_____

_____

_____

_____

_____

If your company culture became toxic, what would that look like? What are some of the warning signs you will look for to ensure toxicity doesn't happen?

What are some elements of a strong values statement? In other words, what are the guiding principles and core beliefs by which your company will operate?

_____

_____

_____

_____

_____

_____

_____

_____

_____

_____

_____

_____

_____

_____

_____

_____

_____

_____

_____

_____

The #1 thing of real importance that leaders do is to create and manage culture…. If you do not manage culture, it manages you, and you may not even be aware of the extent to which this is happening.
— Edgar Schein, professor, MIT Sloan School of Management

SCORING THE GAME:

If you can clearly define culture and values succinctly and *everyone* in the organization embraces this statement, you will greatly increase your odds for competing in the game of business. Assuming you have already completed the exercises in the 1st and 2nd innings, score one run for your team!

If you struggled during this inning, take a breather and replay it again before moving ahead to the next inning. This game isn't a sprint to the finish; be patient and great things will happen….

3rd INNING SCORECARD

What are your key takeaways from this 3rd inning?

_____

_____

_____

_____

_____

_____

_____

_____

_____

_____

_____

_____

_____

_____

_____

_____

_____

_____

Major League Profile – Warren Buffett

Since his early days as a budding investor, Warren Buffett has always maintained a philosophy and culture of value investing. He embraces fundamental values and embodies simple living, both of which have served him well. Buffett is one of the world's richest men, with assets approaching $50 billion. His main source of wealth comes from his company Berkshire Hathaway, a conglomerate holding company that is headquartered in Omaha, Nebraska.

From a very young age, Buffett displayed the characteristics of an entrepreneur and investor. He began by going door to door, selling chewing gum, magazines, and Coca-Cola. In elementary school, he ended up purchasing and placing several pinball machines in different stores.

His entrepreneurial spirit carried through college, and he graduated with sufficient savings to seed several investment partnerships. These partnerships would make him a millionaire through stock ownership. One of the investments was in a textile manufacturing company called Berkshire Hathaway, which he eventually took over and ran.

Subsequent investments in *The Washington Post*, General RE, ABC, Coca-Cola, and Salomon Inc. would make him a billionaire.

Buffett offers three leadership lessons:

1. **Stick to fundamental values:** In an age where there are so many new things, we must learn to stick to fundamental leadership principles of vision, character, and discipline. While theories come and go, principles that govern effective leadership are constant and never changing.

2. **Live simply:** Many leaders are distracted by material possessions, to the point that they sometimes become a distraction to the company vision. Beware of the leader who seeks recognition and reward over pursuing belief in the company mission and vision.

3. **Give back:** As a leader, always remember the reason why one is in leadership—to be an asset to the world, not to take from the world.

PART 2

· ·

The Middle Innings

It's All About Leaders, Teams, Strategy,
Tactics, Execution, Accountability,
and Alignment

4th INNING

Assembling Leaders and Teams—Baseball

STRIVE TO BE A GREAT LEADER

A close friend told me several years ago that a youth baseball coach will never be able to appreciate fully the impact he will have on a young person's life. As a former coach with an adult son, it never ceased to amaze him when former players would come up to thank him for providing such a wonderful experience and awesome memories. My friend also told me that players who have negative experiences with a bad coach live with the consequences of a bad season for many years into the future. Looking back on the past ten years, I have heard countless stories about kids who have given up on team sports, and lost opportunities to learn valuable life lessons about leadership and being part of a team, resulting from having a horrible coach. I have never forgotten my friend's piece of wisdom, and it has served me well. Living into the Little League mission while being a leader, teacher, and positive role model in service to young athletes were primary goals of my baseball coaching.

Imagine if former employees came up to you and expressed their gratitude for having the opportunity at one time to work for your company. Does your business provide the type of environment that makes this possibility a strong likelihood? Would you consider this form of feedback a sign that your leaders and teams are doing the right things?

Alternatively, do you turn away and try to hide when seeing a former employee walking toward you in a crowd? If you feel that way about a former employee, imagine what he or she is saying to others about you and your company. Is this form of *word-of-mouth* what you want spread around the business community?

Imagine the possibilities for you and your company if you were a great leader, 100 percent of the time! That, in my opinion, is a meaningful aspirational goal—one we should all live by.

DEVELOPING FOLLOWERSHIP

Great teams are run by great coaches who know how to: 1) develop a culture where players strive for continuous improvement based on shared values, and 2) develop teams where everyone understands and appreciates his role in the team's success.

The best coaches know how to inspire committed followers to turn a season-long vision into desired outcomes.

Invest time, effort, and money to become someone who inspires followership and you will immediately improve the probability of achieving your baseball goals in a much quicker time frame. The return on this investment will astound you!

SEEING THE BIG PICTURE

In 2009, another coach and I had the privilege of taking a twelve-year-old boys select baseball team to Cooperstown for a week long tournament. There we were, over 100 teams and 2,500 individuals (players, coaches, umpires, and parents) from all over the U.S.A., playing tournament level ball at the birthplace of the game and home of the National Baseball Hall of Fame. I'll talk more about this tournament during the 10th and final inning. By the way, this tournament experience was awesome—if you maintained a view of the big picture!

Let's go back and review the 1st three innings to see what the "big picture" looked like:

1st inning—Definition of Success: A group of twelve-year-old boys were at the birthplace of baseball and home to the National Baseball Hall of Fame to play in a tournament. Come on…does it really get any better?

2nd inning—Why?: Competing in Cooperstown against players from all over the country is the epitome of a youth select baseball tournament experience *and* a memorable summer vacation for families who joined their sons.

3rd inning—Culture and Values: We were blessed to provide everyone involved—players, coaches, and families—with an enjoyable and great learning opportunity.

Now, for a brief description of the "small picture"…

During the entire week, players and coaches lived in a small barracks type building, which had no insulation, no air conditioning, and poor ventilation. The bunk beds squeaked like a bad symphony. Temperatures were in the high 80s to low 90s with matching humidity. Playing two or three games per day led to several injuries, and lots of Icy Hot. Essentially, we lived in a hot, humid, and smelly locker room. And yes, twelve-year-old boys will be twelve-year-old boys. Not a lot of sleeping going on. Needless to say, after the second day, the coaches were starting to get a bit cranky.

The good food and camaraderie were not enough to prevent me from being uncharacteristically snappy a few times during the week. For example, it is easy to get drawn into the weeds so to speak and get upset when a player loses his uniform ten minutes before we are due at the playing field. The other coach was great about helping me gain perspective about the big picture so I would let the little things slide by. I still appreciate his ability to help me relish the entire experience and stay focused on the wonderful week we spent in New York's Catskill Mountains.

Equally, in business, it is important for leaders to maintain a big picture perspective with respect to what is going on within their companies.

INSPIRING FOLLOWERSHIP BY SENDING A STRONG MESSAGE THAT TEAMWORK MATTERS

In 2008, I coached an eleven-year-old All Star baseball team. One boy on that team took delight in pointing out other players' mistakes, probably thinking that by doing so, he would look better by comparison and get more playing time. What he didn't realize was that his behavior not only negatively impacted him and his teammates, but more importantly, it was destructive to the chemistry that is so important for building a great team.

During a water break, I took this young player aside for a brief talk and essentially told him, "You and I will always remember this conversation, but for different reasons. Today happens to be my forty-fifth birthday, and to be perfectly candid, I cannot think of a greater gift than the opportunity to provide you a teachable moment, one that can shape your life in a very positive way. While you are a good person and a fine athlete, there is no room on this team for someone who takes it upon himself to bring his teammates down. What we are trying to do here is take a *team* into a competitive tournament. This group of boys will understand how important each and every person is to the team's success. In order to do our best, we will be supportive of each other going into each practice and game. If you want to be part of this culture and team, I want you to be here. But if that is too difficult for you, then I will ask that you no longer participate."

After a few moments of utter shock, and with tears in his eyes, he said, "Thank you, coach. I understand your point and am glad you were so clear about what you're trying to do." This conversation was never shared with the other team members. But I'm sure they noticed a difference in how the team quickly came together—in an amazing way—after this wonderful and private teachable moment!

In business, events arise where a teachable moment will present itself to you. Do not lose the opportunity to influence positively the outcome of a person's life and your company's health. Be clear that teamwork matters—inspire followership—and your company will reap the rewards!

LEADERS AND MANAGERS

Leadership is doing the right things. Imagine being the type of coach whose players can't wait to come to a practice or game. Such athletes work hard and encourage their teammates. They are sad when the season is over. Chances are that players have these feelings when the coach is a leader they want to follow. The coach has then created a culture that is positive and makes players *want* to be part of the team.

Management is doing things right. In baseball, managing properly means being prepared with a solid practice plan for each week during the season. It also means teaching the game of baseball, at the player and team level, so the technical aspects of position play and game strategy are mastered during the course of a season.

Both leadership and management are responsibilities of the coaching staff. Having said that, how effective would a team be if either leadership or management were weak? When it comes to coaching youth baseball teams, all things being equal, I believe leadership is more important than management.

BUILDING TEAMS

Developing teams takes place on the practice field and in game situations. As a coach, I am constantly looking for ways to improve the way I help players become part of a successful team. The following model was shared with me by Dan Bean, who coaches offense for the freshman high school football team in my hometown. Dan is CEO of a company that serves the airline industry, and he is a great dad who understands the power of positive coaching. The ACE (Anticipate, Communicate, Educate) model is not for bandages—it is for team building!

A̲nticipate: If you are an athlete, baseball is not a spectator sport. Every player on defense should understand exactly what he will do as a play unfolds. Each player should be moving in anticipation of where the ball will be going.

C̲ommunicate: Players should communicate with each other, constantly as each play unfolds. Sometimes, anticipation doesn't put a player in the right place at the right time. There is nothing like constant communication on the field among players to help each other be successful in pursuit of a perfectly executed play.

E̲ducate: Coaches have the opportunity to watch the plays unfold and see what worked well and what didn't. Between innings, a best practice is to spend thirty seconds sharing and educating the players. Positive coaching focuses on helping players understand "what success looks like" and on giving concrete coaching advice for how to achieve mastery in the future.

So in your business, my challenge to you is to think about areas in which the ACE model can be positively applied in pursuit of building a strong team or teams.

INSPIRATION AND POSITIVE ATTITUDE—A WINNING COMBINATION

How often do you inspire others to achieve great things? In other words, what are you doing to turn untapped potential into amazing results in your business? Healthy companies find a way to get the most out of their leaders, who in turn get the most out of their teams.

At the end of the current softball season, I spent some time writing individual thank you notes to each of my players because I so appreciated being part of their success. Do you tell your employees how they inspire you? If not, start doing so.

Below, with the permission of the player's parent—is one of the notes I wrote:

> I wanted to thank you for being part of the team. You are a terrific player and a great teammate.
>
> As a coach, I always look for moments that inspire me. In the past two games, I got that from you!
>
> Two games ago, you were down on yourself because of not being able to get hits at the plate. I said you were a great hitter and took the time to explain why you were—then suggested two things you should focus on while at the plate. You then got a very good hit—a line drive to right field. At first base, you said, "It's about time." I said, "No, that's what you do because you are a good hitter." Your smile at that time could light up the sky!

You were put in a tough position at our final game—having to re-enter the game as pitcher in a tough final inning. It was challenging at best and you were looking a bit down. I yelled out from the dugout, "Be a leader!" Immediately, your body language changed; I saw such determination and mental toughness, and you struck out the next batter and then got another out soon to end the inning. By the way, your hitting in this game was also pretty darn good!

Why will I remember these moments? It is because YOU figured out that greatness lies within you. You were ALWAYS a good hitter, and when reminded to be a great leader, "that's what you did because that's what you do."

Never forget how mental attitude can change outcomes—in sports, in school, and in life. You won't always win, but the odds of doing so greatly improve….

Baseball is just a game—it should be fun to be part of a team—and amazingly—you can learn a few things about yourself along the way.

In reading this note, my challenge to you as a business owner is to take the time to inspire someone each and every week. Your company and the lives of others will benefit immeasurably!

Little League Profile – Leanna Archer

Leanna Archer is learning how to lead and build a sales team to achieve greater success.

At age eleven, Leanna Archer decided to become a hair care mogul. By age twelve, she was named Inc.com Magazine's youngest 30 under 30 Entrepreneur for 2009. She developed and runs Leanna's Natural Hair Products, based in New York.

The products repair damaged hair, using organic formulas passed down through her family for generations and do not contain oil filters, synthetically engineered nor chemically engineered ingredients. From humble beginnings selling to her friends and fellow students, Leanna soon had everyone talking about these amazing products and orders were coming in from stores and online across the U.S. To expand the product line, Leanna invested time to develop new formulations while in middle school.

According to Leanna, "The idea came to me when I received tons of compliments about my hair and I knew it was thanks to my homemade products." She also added, "I had nothing to lose because I figured that if it didn't work out, I still had my whole life ahead of me."

In 2011, the company had revenues of more than $100,000, and revenues are expected to increase to more than $300,000 by the end of 2012. To fuel continued growth, Leanna is in the process of building a team of sales representatives across the United States.

Her advice to small business owners: "All new entrepreneurs should know that mistakes are a big part of success."

ASSEMBLING LEADERS AND TEAMS— BUSINESS

DEVELOPING FOLLOWERSHIP

Great companies are run by great leaders who know how to: 1) develop a success-driven culture based on shared values and 2) build and empower highly functioning teams.

The best leaders *know how* to inspire committed followers to turn company vision into desired outcomes.

They understand that "culture is everything." They are more strategic and see the big picture rather than stay tactical and buried in the proverbial weeds. They also appreciate and actively recognize the contribution each and every person makes who is on their team.

Does this sound like you? If so, you no doubt have greatly improved your odds for achieving business success!

If it does not sound like you, what does not having these leadership skills cost your company every year? Two examples of such costs include *lost profits* from unenthusiastic customers who choose no longer to purchase from your company and the additional expense of *turnover* resulting from losing good employees.

If you invest time, effort, and money to become someone who inspires followership, you will immediately improve the probability of achieving your business goals in a much quicker time frame. The return on this investment will astound you!

Below are ten attributes I believe CEOs can use to inspire followership within their companies:

1. Focus: They have a clear purpose and direction.

2. **Inspiration:** They are someone others *want* to follow.

3. **Proactive Listening:** They proactively seek feedback with a desire for continuous improvement.

4. **Courage:** They make tough decisions.

5. **Transparency:** They say what they mean and mean what they say.

6. **Authenticity:** Whom they are at work is whom they are outside of work.

7. **Forgiving:** They have an ability to hit the "re-set" button, learn from mistakes, and move forward.

8. **Nimble:** They understand that flexibility is a requirement and not an option.

9. **Serve Others:** They go out of their way to ensure that employees can be successful in their roles.

10. **Team Building:** They make sure each and every person in the company is a valued contributor and understands how his or her role can positively or negatively impact results.

Take a good look at the list above and think about what other qualities are important to run your company. Have you done that? If so, congratulations! You're on your way toward developing a leadership scorecard that can help you become a better CEO.

SEEING THE BIG PICTURE

The metaphor of driving a car *really fast* is the closest I know to describing the challenges nearly all CEOs face in getting through the tactical pressures of their daily grind.

Imagine driving down a long stretch of highway at 120 mph on a 3,000-mile road rally. Your focus is narrow—strictly between the white lines—which keep you alive!

That's a good thing, right? Well, maybe not—especially if you are heading in the wrong direction!

Sticking with the driving metaphor, when focus is tactical, strictly on the immediate, furiously trying to make good time, big problems can occur. Driving in the wrong direction is a possible outcome. So is driving off a cliff!

So what's the point of this metaphor? In two words: BE STRATEGIC! Do not allow yourself to fall into the "tactical trap" of the daily grind so much that you lose sight of your #1 goal as CEO—to define clearly your company's vision and strategy, while enabling your leaders, managers, and other employees to move the business in that direction.

In road rallies, there is always a co-driver who serves as navigator while looking several miles ahead with his binoculars for potential bumps in the road. A CEO would do well to have a strong team of people helping to lead his company toward clearly defined strategic goals and a destination.

SENDING A STRONG MESSAGE THAT TEAMWORK MATTERS

Do you work toward building a team of employees throughout the entire organization who share and embrace your company's vision and values? Remember that stronger alignment always produces a better outcome!

Would you employ a "star performer" who was a horrible fit for your company culture? What is the right thing to do if you're trying to build enterprise value in your company?

Most people would agree that successful CEOs need to do two things right in order to build a valuable company: 1) clearly articulate the vision, and 2) ensure the leadership and management team successfully executes on that vision.

LEADERS AND MANAGERS

Below is the BIG difference between leadership and management.

1. Leadership is doing the right things.

2. Management is doing things right.

Great leaders don't necessarily make great managers.

Great managers don't necessarily make great leaders.

EMPLOYEES ARE NOT CREATED EQUAL

If you want outcomes to improve dramatically in your company, build an action plan based on the idea that *Employees are NOT Created Equal.*

Start by taking time to separate your employees into three categories:

1. **Actively disengaged:** These employees are hindering your company in a big way. They are disruptive to customers, vendors, or co-workers. If you were evil and wanted to destroy a strong company, its culture or teams, you'd look for these people as your go-to individuals.

2. **Going through the motions:** Most employees fall into this category. They are comfortable with and competent in their work, show up and participate when asked, but could be accurately described as biding their time until something better comes along.

3. **Actively engaged:** These employees are passionate about their work and strive to improve dramatically the experiences of customers and co-workers, transforming ordinary results into extraordinary outcomes.

Now that you've put your employees into three different categories, let's discuss the next steps:

1. **Actively disengaged employees:** Take a moment and add up the total compensation and benefits you are paying to *actively disengaged employees.* Then add to that the spillover costs resulting from customers who decide to buy from a competitor along with high performing employees who leave your company seeking a better working environment. Now ask yourself, "How long am I willing to continue paying the cost of employing these *active-*

ly disengaged individuals?" My advice is to stop it and get rid of those who are cancerous to your company. Until challenged, many CEOs won't do this—they will have all kinds of reasons to maintain the status quo. Remember, there is a cost for doing nothing....

2. **Going through the motions:** Invest the time to lead and inspire these employees to become *actively engaged.* Building a healthy company culture is most important. In addition, clarifying how the employee is important to the company's success, and then providing recognition and reward when he behaves and performs in ways consistent with your company culture and goals can build *active engagement* in short time!

3. **Actively engaged employees:** What are you doing to attract and retain these key performers? What is your plan? Is it effective? What needs to change? What needs to stay the same?

Big picture—the goal is simple. Weed out your *disengaged employees* while inspiring your remaining employees to become or remain *actively engaged.* The results will astound you!

Let's review key takeaways before I give you a practice drill to work on.

A great leader:

1. Is someone others want to follow. Great leaders inspire followership!

2. Sees the big picture. The big picture is important if you are going to lead a company in the right direction.

3. Sends a strong message that team work matters.

4. Knows the difference between leaders and managers. Makes sure he has the right people in the right roles.

5. Is deliberate in how his team is built. He uses his company culture as a guide.

Okay. Now it is time to continue writing in your game plan journal and to answer the following questions to develop leadership and teams:

What do you do to inspire followership in your company? What could you do better?

_____

_____

_____

_____

_____

_____

_____

_____

_____

_____

_____

_____

_____

_____

_____

_____

_____

Are you clearly focused on the few essential things necessary to build a thriving company? Are you juggling too many balls, most of which are non-essential? What are the essential few? What can be lowered in priority? What can be taken off the list entirely?

_____

_____

_____

_____

_____

_____

_____

_____

_____

_____

_____

_____

_____

_____

_____

_____

What is your game plan for building strong leaders and teams? What is working and what needs to change?

_____

_____

_____

_____

_____

_____

_____

_____

_____

_____

_____

_____

_____

_____

_____

_____

_____

_____

Do you have the right people in leadership and management roles? What are you doing to help develop their strengths and mitigate their weaknesses?

_____

_____

_____

_____

_____

_____

_____

_____

_____

_____

_____

_____

_____

_____

_____

_____

_____

_____

Are you strictly focused on what's immediately in front of you, or are you instead proactively guiding your car in the right direction?
— James Whitfield, President, Leadership Eastside

SCORING THE GAME

If you are a leader whom others want to follow and you see the big picture, congratulations!—you have runners at 2nd and 3rd base. If you have identified weaknesses among your leadership and management and have a plan in place to build strong teams, then you have scored a run!

If you struggled during this inning, don't worry. Take the time to develop strong leaders and teams. This work is important because it will enable you to come out ahead at the end of this game.

4th INNING SCORECARD

What are your key takeaways from this 4th inning?

_____

_____

_____

_____

_____

_____

_____

_____

_____

_____

_____

_____

_____

_____

_____

_____

Major League Profile – Andrew Carnegie

Andrew Carnegie is famous for acknowledging that one's success as a leader is completely dependent on the quality of his team.

In the nineteenth century, Carnegie was the father of modern steel and one of America's richest men. He founded Carnegie Steel Company, which later merged with Steel Company to become U.S. Steel.

With wealth created from his company and investments in railroad-related businesses, Carnegie started his philanthropic work at the age of sixty-six and started many foundations and organizations for the causes of world peace, education, and libraries. Carnegie Hall in New York City was named after him.

Carnegie offered three leadership lessons:

1. **The value of hard work**: In the modern day world of instant gratification, it is important never to lose sight of the principle that hard work and effort lead to success. Victory is hard-earned, and as a leader, you need to embody hard work and lead your team in a similar manner to see success come to your organization.

2. **It is not what you know but whom you know**: In business, you cannot do it alone. Whatever you hope to achieve in life, you need good people around you. It's not about knowing as much as possible, but instead knowing as many people as possible.

   Andrew Carnegie understood this principle and purposefully went all out to meet people of prominence whenever he had the chance.

3. Give back: It is important to live your life to give and to teach your team to live a life to give. With this attitude, you will succeed at becoming someone of significance in life.

At the age of thirty-three and achieving tremendous financial success, Carnegie found great emptiness in his life of riches, which is when he realized that a life lived solely for self was an empty life.

5ᵗʰ INNING

Developing Strategy and
Tactically Executing The Plan—Baseball

Congratulations! By now, you have developed your leaders and teams, defined the culture of a successful youth baseball program, have a very clear understanding about why boys sign up to play youth baseball, and have defined what success looks like.... Now, it is time to start developing a winning strategy and execute your tactical plan for your upcoming season.

Since what we are doing is building a successful youth program, every coach and manager should be working from an identical template for both strategic and tactical execution plans. The desired outcome is a positive experience for all players on all teams, and the easiest way to get there is to have all teams aligned with the league's culture, strategic goals, and tactical objectives.

The following paragraphs show how a league could operate with two strategic goals, each goal having three tactical steps to support it.

DEVELOP STRATEGY AND TACTICS—WITH THE END IN MIND

The league has established two strategic goals:

1. Turn players and parents into advocates for youth baseball, with a 95 percent return rate for players in the following year.

2. Build a very competitive program that does well in playoffs and All Stars.

If the youth baseball board of directors, team managers, and coaches are successful in accomplishing these two goals, the program should always have a pipeline of players and become a thriving and sustainable program.

Below are examples of how tactical execution steps can be developed in support of each strategic goal:

Strategic Goal #1: Turn players into advocates for youth baseball, with a 95 percent return rate for players in the following year.

The following three tactical steps are defined to support the first strategic objective.

1. Create a fun and competitive environment, where the focus is on building a team and strengthening friendships.

2. Make practices instructional and competitive.

3. Offer consistent positive reinforcement and opportunities to make good plays, knowing that boys need to play well in order to feel good about themselves.

Strategic Goal #2: Build a very competitive program that does well in playoffs and All Stars.

1. Discover how other youth programs build successful programs. Replicate what works, discard what doesn't work, and add what else is needed.

2. Keep track of what each player needs to improve. Deliberately practice and develop skill in areas of weakness, and don't spend a

lot of time focusing on what the players are already proficient at doing.

3. Build a progressive program for the entire season, where there is a well-constructed plan for each practice and a new skill or strategy to introduce in each game.

Since I mentioned deliberate practice, it makes sense to spend a bit of time explaining what it really means.

TACTICAL EXECUTION—DELIBERATE PRACTICE

What NOT to do: When taking players through batting practice, many coaches often throw their pitches down the middle of the plate, waist high. This pitch teaches batters how to hit baseballs thrown in the sweet spot. They quickly develop the timing and swing to crush baseballs and think they are good hitters. This practice can help a player achieve a high level of self-confidence, but it doesn't serve the player or team very well.

Unfortunately, pitchers in game situations do not often cooperate by throwing balls down the middle of the plate, so hitters become discouraged and lose whatever confidence they have gained. This process is not anything close to the concept of deliberate practice.

What to do: The principle of deliberate practice requires coaches to work proactively with their players on improving what needs improving—NOT what a player is already good at doing.

For example, if you want players to become better hitters:

1. Help them figure out which pitches and locations are easier for them to hit. In game situations, until they develop mastery else-

where, waiting for a pitch they can hit well is what they should be looking for on zero and one strike situations.

2. During practice, spend nearly 100 percent of the time teaching each player how to become more proficient, hitting other types of pitches and locations where they currently struggle. Players get better through instruction, repetition, and learning how to develop the mental toughness necessary to become good hitters.

3. Keep practicing until each player achieves some level of success from learning something new. Give each player positive reinforcement and explain why he did well. Encourage development of mental and muscle memory so each athlete can begin the process of training his brain and body to learn new skills and become a better hitter.

With regard to your company, what are the things you are doing to help employees elevate their games so they better serve customers and each other? Is this process deliberate or haphazard? Spend some time thinking about how to help your employees be successful; as a result of their becoming better employees, they in turn will help you be successful.

One of my favorite parts of each baseball season is teaching players the connection between how a team practices and how it plays in a game.

TACTICAL EXECUTION—PRACTICE MAKES PERMANENT

Here's a question for you youth coaches and leaders out there. Are you, as the manager/coach, bringing the best out in your team? If not, get started—elevating your team habits leads to dramatically improved results—every time!

Over the past ten years, I've coached twenty-eight youth sports teams—you could say coaching is a passion of mine. At the beginning of each season, one of the first things I ask players is, "Practice makes ___?" Almost everyone shouts out "PERFECT!" Those who have been on my prior teams shake their heads and say, "No—the answer is PERMANENT!"

This question comes up in practice when the players are looking particularly unfocused and going through the motions. They know their performance level is less than their potential. It is disheartening to watch them because while they are practicing, they are in no way working toward perfection. With a smile, I ask whether their current practice habits will lead toward mastery of their position and the game. With many quizzical looks, they start to pay attention. So, "Practice DOES NOT make perfect."

As part of this team talk, I ask the players to envision elements of the perfect game, whether it is aggressive base running, solid team defense, or being great at bats. Then I ask them whether what they are doing at practice comes close to resembling what they envision perfection to look like. The answer is always a resounding "NO!" Then I prophetically state "The way we practice is the way we will play." Now, the metaphorical lightbulbs start flashing like a fireworks display! So "Practice DOES make permanent!"

Then I'll suggest, "If practicing without intensity, focus, and desire to do our best isn't getting us the results we want, what do you think would happen if we all focused, learned from our mistakes, and got better together?" Needless to say, the second half of practice looks nothing like the first half. It is fun, inspiring, and rewarding to experience this lesson in action—it never gets old!

So take this story and apply it to the business world—your company—your team—and its practice habits. Are the habits of highly successful organizations being developed within your organization? Do your employees work toward achieving mastery of their spheres of influence in the company? Or do they instead go through the motions, thinking that success will arrive if they simply show up for work? Be purposeful in your pursuit of success! After all, potentially millions of dollars in company value are at stake.

Here's what I'd like you to take away from this concept:

1. Clearly define what success looks like.

2. Compare it to where you are today.

3. Develop a detailed plan to fill the gap.

Begin the process of deliberate practice and execute your plan with an intensity that comes with knowing the game is on the line—because it is!

Little League Profile – Fraser Doherty

Developing a business strategy and tactically executing on these objectives is what enabled Fraser Doherty to capture 10 percent of the market for jams in his home country.

In 2002, at age fourteen, Fraser Doherty started making jams from his grandmother's recipe. His first production facility was in his parents' kitchen in Edinburgh, Scotland. Friends and neighbors kept buying his jams and spreading the word. Fraser was about to find out how positive word-of-mouth would impact his business. Before too long, Fraser was receiving orders faster than he could produce at home so he decided it was time to rent a 200-person food processing facility for a few days each month.

Two years later at age sixteen, Fraser left school with his parents' blessing and worked on building his company full-time. At the ripe old age of seventeen, a high-end supermarket approached Fraser about selling his SuperJam in their stores. Before too long, SuperJam could be found on the shelves of 184 stores, taking the business to a whole new level.

Fraser had to borrow some money to cover general expenses and more factory time. Other grocery store companies started to bring in SuperJam until now the products are carried in 300 stores throughout the UK and Ireland.

In 2007, SuperJam achieved $750,000 in sales, and it doubled that number in 2008, which translates to about 50,000 jars each month. Based on a reasonable valuation multiple of one times revenue, at that point in time, Fraser's company was worth between $1 million and $2 million. That's pretty good for a nineteen-year-old.

Fast forward to 2012, and SuperJam is now sold in The Netherlands, France, Germany, and Australia.

Fraser's advice to other entrepreneurs is, "Have an attitude of adventure, and enjoy the journey."

Developing Strategy and Tactically Executing The Plan—Business

DEVELOP STRATEGY AND TACTICS—WITH THE END IN MIND

Many companies go through a strategic planning process and find it to be a complete waste of time and money. Others find the experience to be the single most important action taken to build very successful and valuable companies. Years of experience with multiple companies has enabled me to see both outcomes. Before exploring why two different outcomes can result, here are some thoughts to consider:

A good Strategic Plan provides a roadmap between where your company is today and where it should be in the future.

A good Strategic Planning Process enables all stakeholders to align themselves to organizational goals. Inclusive process and transparent communication is important.

The Strategic Plan and Strategic Planning Process are both equally important.

After helping develop multiple strategic plans, I've come up with several essential elements that produce good outcomes:

1. Define the gap: Acknowledge your company's current position/ condition and articulate a vision for some point in the future (three years works well). The "gap" is the puzzle your strategic plan seeks to solve.

2. Obtain employee "Buy-In": Build a bottom up approach to allow employees to participate and share their observations and recommendations *before* imposing your ideas (as owner/CEO) on

the team. This buy-in will emotionally connect employees to the plan—which is a big deal!

3. Agree on the essential few key initiatives that will move the company forward toward its goals.

4. Agree on a tactical plan for each strategic initiative and assign accountability and collaboration partners responsible for execution.

5. Communicate and share widely, at least quarterly. Monitor, measure, and share progress on plan execution in order to build understanding and alignment throughout the entire company.

6. As business conditions dictate, periodically revisit whether undertaking a new strategic planning process makes sense.

7. Good strategic plans are dynamic, periodically reviewed, and widely shared.

TACTICAL EXECUTION—DELIBERATE PRACTICE AND PROCESS

Great CEOs and business owners know where they are guiding their businesses. A well-designed strategic plan is like their flight plan. A well-designed strategic planning process will ensure employee alignment and buy-in with the flight plan.

Taking a plane into the air without having a flight plan is a bad idea. Trying to run a company without its leaders and employees knowing where it is going and how it is going to get there is also a bad idea.

While I agree it's critical to develop long-range strategic business plans, along with shorter term tactical action plans that support the business strategy, neither matters if a leader cannot execute on his plan.

My question is: Do you have an execution plan to support the strategic and tactical plans for your business?

If a leadership team is going to "Get 'er done," it needs to have certain elements:

Each strategic initiative and tactical action item needs an individual to be accountable and responsible for completion.

Collaboration teams need to be identified, developed, and nurtured.

A plan/process of getting from "Point A to Point B" must be established.

Progress needs to be periodically measured and assessed.

Tracking progress may also require implementing a Plan B when Plan A is not working.

Managing execution risk means identifying what can go wrong and being ready to act when bad things happen.

Dashboards are a great way to track and measure progress on strategic, tactical, and execution plans. The mistake many companies make is to build dashboards that only look at past financial results. Great dashboards also measure and track behaviors that lead to value-enhancing activities and businesses successfully executing their plans.

THE DIFFERENCE BETWEEN INVESTMENT AND COST

When determining the best way to spend money in your company, I think business owners should forget everything the CFO or Controller says about defining the difference between investment and cost.

Accountants will tell you "Investments get capitalized on the balance sheet, and costs flow through as an expense on the income statement.

In other words, property, plant, and equipment, along with goodwill made in conjunction with company acquisitions are *investments*. Everything else pretty much is a *cost* or expense."

My definition of a good investment is: "Spending time and money in a particular area that provides an improved business outcome such that the value received is dramatically higher than any time and money spent."

My advice is to identify where investments in both time and money provide great value toward building a more profitable and sustainable company. Let me give you two examples:

1. If you need help building a stronger and more profitable company and want to find a way to spend less time doing it, invest time and money to get it done. The absence of this action guarantees you a lower standard of living in terms of lost value, income, and discretionary time.

2. If you do not know which areas of your company are profitable and not profitable, and you do not get actionable financial information every month that can help you better lead the business, then invest the time and money to get this done. Running your company blindly is dangerous and risky.

In both instances, the cost of doing nothing is usually a very high number resulting from lower profits and cash flow.

Let's review key takeaways before I give you practice exercises to work on.

1. Define the gap between the current state and desired state of your company. This gap becomes the goal/objective of developing and executing a strategic business plan.

2. Collaboratively build the plan with input and buy-in from your employees. They need to be emotionally invested in the plan in order for it to work.

3. Periodically review progress and continually communicate with your employees about progress or lack of progress. Employees are your partners in success. Engage them well....

Okay. Now it is time to continue writing in your game plan journal, and to answer the following questions to develop business strategy and a tactical execution plan:

Now that you are actively engaging with your team at work, redefine your definitions of success. Have they changed since the first inning?

_____

_____

_____

_____

_____

_____

_____

_____

_____

_____

_____

_____

_____

_____

_____

_____

_____

_____

_____

How does this definition of success look different from your business today? Be specific. Define the gap. Filling in what is missing becomes the goal of your strategic plan.

_____

_____

_____

_____

_____

_____

_____

_____

_____

_____

_____

_____

_____

_____

_____

_____

_____

_____

_____

_____

Spend time with your employees, solicit their thoughts, and build consensus and buy-in for their participation in the process. Who needs to be involved? How long will it take?

_____

_____

_____

_____

_____

_____

_____

_____

_____

_____

_____

_____

_____

_____

_____

_____

_____

_____

_____

_____

Agree on the essential few strategic goals that will move the company to your definition of success. What are they? Who needs to be involved? How long will it take?

Develop a tactical plan for each strategic initiative and assign accountability and collaboration partners responsible for execution. What are the strategic initiatives? Who needs to be involved? How long will it take?

_____

_____

_____

_____

_____

_____

_____

_____

_____

_____

_____

_____

_____

_____

_____

_____

_____

_____

Take the time now to mark your calendar to communicate with your employees on a quarterly basis. Monitor, measure, and share progress on plan execution in order to build understanding and alignment throughout the entire company. Who will make arrangements and hold you accountable for following up?

On an annual basis, review whether the business environment has changed sufficiently enough to warrant undertaking another strategic planning process.

Executives' good intentions and words, like their companies' stocks, lose their value when nothing backs them up.
— Al Watts, author of *Navigating Integrity: Transforming Business As Usual Into Business At Its Best*

SCORING THE GAME

If you have collaboratively developed a strategic business plan with tactical execution steps in support of your business strategy, congratulations—you have base runners in scoring position!

If your employees embrace their places in your "game of business" and are truly in support of your goals, you will start scoring runs and it is going to be a good inning!

If you failed to bring in employees and develop your plan from the ground up, grab your glove and go out and play defense. Sorry, you aren't going to score any runs this inning....

5TH INNING SCORECARD

What are your key takeaways from this inning?

_____

_____

_____

_____

_____

_____

_____

_____

_____

_____

_____

_____

_____

_____

_____

_____

_____

_____

_____

_____

Major League Profile – John D. Rockefeller

Many leaders strategically plan to grow their businesses by acquiring their competitors. John D. Rockefeller did just that through his Standard Oil Company, which began acquiring many of its competitors and became the largest oil supplier in the U.S. Rockefeller successfully convinced many of his competitors that it was unprofitable to compete against him.

As a result of successful execution of this business strategy, John D. Rockefeller became the first billionaire in world history. In today's dollars, Rockefeller is still considered the richest man in modern history. Eventually, the Standard Oil Company was deemed to be monopolistic and was separated into thirty-four different companies, some of which still exist today in the form of ExxonMobil, BP, and Chevron.

Later in life, Rockefeller was one of the world's few great philanthropists, and after retirement, he spent his time giving back a huge portion of his wealth to society, funding the University of Chicago and many forms of medical research.

Rockefeller offered three leadership lessons:

1. **Shrewdness:** As a leader, we must learn to be wise in dealing with other people. While important to maintain integrity and character, it is also important to be shrewd when dealing with people we are not sure about. Within an organization, you must have mutual trust. However, outside the organization, not everyone

has your best interests at heart. Learn to be wise and careful with the people with whom you are dealing.

Rockefeller almost always managed to come out a winner in the deals he made.

2. **Focus not on money but instead on character and reputation:** As a leader, do not be seduced by the pursuit of money at the cost of destroying your reputation and character. When chasing money, people run away from you and so does the money. Build a solid reputation and money will follow you wherever you go.

3. **Give back to society:** The true source of wealth comes from a capacity to give. We have to adopt the same attitude of giving. Money is the expression of our heart and attitude. As a leader, we must embrace the attitude of a giver and not a taker.

6th INNING

Creating Alignment—Baseball

ALIGNMENT AND VELOCITY

Alignment equals velocity. The more aligned a youth baseball team becomes, the more likely the team will have a great season and the more likely the kids will want to play again next year. "So what is alignment?" you ask. Let me try to explain...first with what is not alignment.

If one definition of success is to have kids tell their friends what a great season they had playing baseball, but 30 percent of the coaches are more concerned about winning games without regard to whether players are developing as people and athletes or having a good time being part of the team, then you have a classic case of misalignment.

So if alignment is the goal, it becomes important to figure out where the team is NOT aligned, and then come up with a game plan to fix what needs fixing. To help visualize how this can work, below is a simple illustration of a two-dimensional assessment tool that a team manager can use at any given time to assess the level of alignment on a youth baseball team:

	Manager	Coach	Players	Parents
Culture	Green	Green	Yellow	Red
Strategy	Green	Green	Yellow	Yellow
Tactics	Green	Green	Green	Green

139

The color coding system works similarly to a traffic light system: green is good, yellow is cautionary, and red is bad.

Vertical alignment assesses, at any particular level on the team, how culture is aligned with its strategy for the baseball season, and with its tactical plan for building team chemistry, along with team and individual player development.

Horizontal alignment assesses how the team, from an organizational perspective, is able to function within the parameters of vertical alignment. Using the example above, the manager and coach are in complete alignment with respect to the team's culture, strategy, and tactics for the season. The players and parents need help in the areas of culture and strategy. Maximum velocity occurs when both vertical and horizontal alignment exist.

The paragraphs below describe how a youth baseball program might establish season-long goals for everyone involved with the team's culture, strategy, and tactics.

CULTURE

1. Coaches are uniformly trained to serve the athletes by providing a fun environment in a positive culture.

2. Coaches are supported by other coaches, parents, fans, umpires, and athletes—all of whom learn to compete while honoring the game and its rules.

3. Every athlete has an important role to play on the team. Not everyone will be a star performer, but all athletes can contribute to the team's success. Coaches take time to recognize successful behavior. Each athlete feels valued as an important team member.

4. Coaches and athletes learn life lessons from their experiences during each game and the season.

5. Athletes, parents, and fans have an awesome experience and tell all of their friends!

STRATEGY

1. Early season focus is on developing team chemistry and assessing strengths and weaknesses.

2. Mid-season focus is on developing mental toughness and player skill development.

3. Late season focus is on developing ability to be competitive and win close games.

4. Post-season focus is on winning the post-season tournament.

TACTICS

1. During the early season, a significant amount of time is spent building team chemistry. Coaches spend a lot of time upfront getting players and parents up to speed on team culture. Practices focus on rotating drill stations to give every player opportunities to showcase his abilities and highlight areas for improvement. High energy and high effort practices are rewarded with a team drill contest at the end. Prizes are awarded if the team is success-ful—ice cream and pizza are great motivators.

2. During the mid-season, players start focusing on developing mastery at primary and secondary defensive positions. The bat-ting line-up is getting developed based on each player's ability to contribute to offense. The concept of "pressure" is applied in

practice, in both practice drills and game simulation, with the idea of helping athletes learn how to play a game and minimize how a pressure situation will impact their ability to play at their maximum capability.

3. During the late season, the focus is on the "little things" that make big differences: game strategy, learning how to play "small ball" and manufacture a run with the weak part of the batting line-up, learning how to shave $3/10^{ths}$ of a second off each defensive play, and continuing the journey of developing mental toughness among all players on the team.

4. During the post-season, everyone on the team understands his role, knows what is expected of him, and knows how to be both a great teammate and athlete. Game plans are developed and executed well because months of deliberate practice made a great team.

HOW MISALIGNMENT OCCURS

Below are some examples of how misalignment can exist at the manager, coach, player, or parent level:

Manager/coach: Some managers/coaches use their leadership roles to put their sons in positions that are not best for the team. Often, they also view the team's win/loss record as a personal reflection on their ability to coach and exclusively play the best players in order to win games and stroke their egos. The most frequent example of this misalignment is using a strong pitcher early in the season to the point that he injures his throwing arm late in the season.

Player: Some players get it into their heads that they are either too good to be on the team or not good enough. Neither is true, and both types of attitude are detrimental to a team's ability to succeed. Players who think "When am I going to get an opportunity to show everyone what I can do and show off in front of others?" don't make good teammates. Their egos usually get too big and nobody on the team wants to be around them. Players who think "I am terrible and shouldn't be out here" not only enable their lack of confidence to become a self-fulfilling prophecy that results in poor performance, but their teammates will not be supportive of someone who doesn't believe in his abilities. Conversely, nothing inspires a team more than the player who finds a way to over-perform relative to his defined "capability." Success breeds more success—the "virtuous cycle." Inversely, the *Vortex of Doom* occurs when one bad thing leads to another—with no end in sight.

Parent: I cannot imagine the pressure young athletes feel when their parents take the game too seriously—okay, a LOT too seriously. I've heard the craziest things come out of parents' mouths, such as "Don't strike out and disappoint me!" Hmmm, what do you think is going to happen when a nervous player hears that his parent will be disappointed in him if he strikes out? Chances are, that's ALL he is thinking about, so it becomes a self-fulfilling prophecy. I've heard parents scream at their sons, teammates, coaches, and umpires, all over a kid's game. If you cannot understand how screaming can cause misalignment, go back and re-read the last two pages. There isn't room for that behavior in a program meant to produce a positive outcome for the kids we are all serving!

Now take a moment and think about how these examples serve or do not serve as a metaphor for what shows up in your business. The lack of alignment is costing your business a lot of lost profits and value. It's time to make changes necessary to capture and realize that value.

HOW TO CREATE ALIGNMENT

A youth baseball team is comprised of a manager, coach, players, and parents. Collectively, this is "the team." Building a great team with complete alignment requires a commitment to being 100 percent clear, transparent, fair, inspirational, and motivational. By keeping everyone on the team focused on *why* the kids are playing baseball, the definition of team success, team culture, and being a leader others want to follow, you will create the alignment necessary to execute quickly on the strategic and tactical plans for your baseball season.

Little League Profile – Mark Bao

Mark Bao provides a great example of how building alignment among various business ventures accelerates growth and success.

At age nineteen, Mark can be described as a successful serial technology entrepreneur. He has sold three web companies, two of which were highly profitable. One reached over 250,000 subscribers within three weeks of initial launch. These ventures, all self-funded, included 1) a social media site called threewords.me, where visitors described their friends' personalities in three words, 2) Facebook Idol, an *American Idol* type of competition app, and 3) Atomplan, a small business management tool.

As Mark says, "I've always been interested in technology and how it can make a difference. Entrepreneurial action creates change." With his entrepreneurial fire burning, Mark has a new self-funded startup called Supportbreeze, a customer service platform that helps businesses manage their support inquiries. This platform is so valuable because the service dramatically cuts down on response time and manpower. The idea for this business came from the realization that Mark needed a really good customer service application for his other startups.

Currently, Mark can be found splitting his time between Supportbreeze, attending college classes, and assisting a friend as Chief Technology Officer at Onswipe, a tablet publishing platform that provides content publishers a user-friendly and beautiful way to display their media and advertising on touch devices.

As for his secret to success, Mark explains, "When you're young, don't fear failing. Whether you succeed or fail, the things you learn will be incredibly valuable for your future endeavors."

Creating Alignment—Business

ALIGNMENT AND VELOCITY

Alignment equals velocity. The more aligned your company is from top to bottom, the quicker you will be able to achieve your definition of success. Another way of saying this is: If your entire organization is not aligned, how much time and money does this cost your business?

To use a metaphor from another sport that illustrates complete alignment, imagine being part of an eight-member crew team that has trained together for several years and is rowing in a calm lake, cutting through the water with everyone moving in complete unison, at thirty-three strokes per minute. From above, the boat and crew team would look like *poetry in motion* and the epitome of a team in complete alignment.

Now imagine a very different scenario, where the lake has very choppy waters, the crew team is brand new, and two of the eight rowers have never participated in the sport; they are out of shape and have no talent. The other six rowers, who are quite talented, are upset to be part of this misaligned team so they go out of their way to row out of sync with the two new rowers, who are doing their best but are ill-suited for this sport. From above, this boat and crew team would look like "a fish out of water" and a stark example of a team in utter disarray.

One way of transforming this unsuccessful crew team into a winning team in the shortest amount of time possible is to build alignment among everyone on the team and find a way to row in calm waters.

To get you thinking about alignment in a business sense, I'd like to share below my business philosophy, describing my personal values and culture, and how they align with business strategy and tactics.

147

Alignment, which is all about getting everyone moving in the same direction, is critical if you want to be expeditious in getting from where your business currently is positioned to where you want it to be in the future.

CULTURE

I like to think of *culture* in business as the container within which a company operates. Containers can be healthy, toxic, or somewhere in-between. *Strategy* is a long-term plan of action to achieve your business goals and objectives. *Tactics* are short-term steps taken to achieve a business strategy. Below is a brief explanation of how culture aligns with strategy and tactics.

To begin, culture in my business is best described by always aspiring to create value with everyone I meet. I accomplish this goal by always listening, learning, and then determining how best to add value to every person in every conversation. The idea of putting other people's interests first and continually adding value to their lives ultimately leads to unexpected success. Some call this process a *virtuous cycle*, where doing good for others leads to good being done unto you. I call it the *circle of success*—and this philosophy and *culture* is a core value of mine.

Conversely, the opposite type of people are self-described "go-takers"—so ambitious that they will destroy those in their way in their pursuit of their definition of success. These same people will take what they want without regard for others and then later beg for forgiveness—with the self-satisfaction of accomplishing another one of their goals. I guess this individualized culture works—as many embrace it. But it doesn't align with the way I work; nor will it align with those with whom I choose to work.

STRATEGY

Aligned with my *culture* is a business strategy of building positive word-of-mouth—or advocacy—which is a simple way of saying I want to create an environment where others are proactively saying good things about me and my business to other people. It seems obvious that having others say good things about me is going to be a lot more effective than me going around saying stuff like "I'm a pretty amazing guy, and if you don't believe me, just ask and I'll tell you!" First of all, that isn't my style—AT ALL. Secondly, if I'm successful in doing enough things to earn positive word-of-mouth, then I will receive feedback that I'm doing the *right* things to grow my business.

TACTICS

The primary business tactic that supports and aligns with my strategy and culture is to share information openly with the intent of serving while recognizing that I don't have all the answers but am humble enough to work toward finding workable solutions by engaging the help of others. Lenora Edwards, a business development advisor to consultants, coined the concept "the Reese's Peanut Butter Cup effect," where two individuals—metaphorically chocolate and peanut butter—come together in a collaborative way to create a solution greater than what would have been possible as individuals.

Whether it be writing a book or blogging, speaking to CEO groups, or freely sharing ideas through networking meetings, my tactical plan is to attract those who find what I offer valuable—in a *pull* fashion—so they actively seek my products and/or consulting services. This strategy is diametrically opposed to active *push* marketing and selling to individuals who may or may not be interested in what I have to offer.

THE NORDSTROM EXAMPLE

If you want to reduce the amount of time it takes to increase value in your company in dramatic ways—align company culture and values with strategy and tactical execution. That's a fancy way of saying: Get everyone in your business figuratively "rowing in the same direction—on multiple levels." This simple idea can be very complex and difficult work, but the rewards will astound you! Consider it one of the "essential few" things that can significantly improve business outcomes and reduce personal headaches.

Nordstrom has a culture that values superior customer service. Everyone in the company rallies around that principle—from the floor salesperson up to the CEO. Can you and everyone in your company define in one or two sentences what your company's culture and values are? If not, why not? If everyone can, congratulations! You've developed cultural alignment!

I'm guessing that part of Nordstrom's business strategy is to build customer advocates—people who RAVE about the Nordstrom shopping experience to their friends. Having others say good things about you is a lot more powerful than self-promotion. Can you articulate your business strategy in very simple and understandable terms? Can everyone at all levels in your company do so (in relation to his or her sphere of influence)? If not, why not? If you can say, "Yes," then congratulations! You've developed strategic alignment!

At the tactical level, Nordstrom empowers its salespeople to make decisions in support of the company culture and business strategy. Not a lot of micro-managing is going on when it comes to delivering the awesome customer experience. Nordstrom employees "get it"! Are your employees tactically executing at the ground level in alignment with how you see the company moving at the 30,000-foot level? If you cannot answer this question, why not? If the answer is "No," why not? If you can say, "Yes," then congratulations! You've created tactical alignment!

If you answered "Yes," "Yes," and "Yes" to the questions above, congratulations! You have the makings of a very healthy company. With one or more "No" answers, it's time to seek "chiropractic adjustments" for the health of your business.

Following are two key questions you can ask yourself to start developing an action plan: 1) What changes, if any, need to be made within my company culture to provide a sound container capable of supporting tactical execution of my business strategy? 2) What changes, if any, need to be made to my organization chart, strategically and tactically, from top to bottom, to align with company culture?

Let's review a few key thoughts before moving to the final section of this inning.

1. Alignment equals velocity.

2. Achieving your business goals will happen much quicker if your company culture is aligned with business strategy and tactics.

3. Alignment needs to take place at all levels in your company.

ALIGN THE LANGUAGE TO GROW YOUR BUSINESS

Externally generated language happens when others do the talking for your business. Deliver great value to your customers and they will be telling others to do business with your company.

Internally generated language happens when your employees do the talking for your business. Many companies have business development professionals or sales teams that extol their employer's virtues to potential customers—to bring in new revenue.

When aligning your company's language to grow your business, consider these questions:

Are external and internal language aligned? If not, why not? Are you comfortable that customers may be saying things differently from your business development team? Do you even know what customers are saying about their experiences with your company?

Is internal language aligned among your business development team?

Misaligned language is confusing—and that's bad for business! To illustrate, below are a couple of ways misaligned language can show up:

Customers say bad things about your company, but your business development team says otherwise. If this misalignment happens, you've got the opposite of business development going on—welcome to the wheel of pain—where one bad thing leads to another—and ultimately loss of customers, profits, and value. To solve this problem, invest time and money to become better at serving your customers, and if necessary, spend less time and money in business development. In other words, fix the customer experience problem before adding more fuel to the fire.

Your business development team is inconsistent in how it talks about your company. In the past two weeks, I've met with business development professionals who did a great job describing their company—but it sounded NOTHING like what my impression was based on talking with others who work at the same company. I'm sure others like me are confused based on this inconsistent language. That's not good! To solve this problem, bring the team together, provide clarity regarding your company's authentic business language, role play meetings with customer and prospects, and adapt and adopt best practices while creating alignment of message.

My challenge to you is simple to state but difficult to implement: Will you invest the time to define what you want to be said about your company, and then go about creating external and internal alignment in your business language?

Okay. Now it is time to continue writing in your game plan journal and to answer the following questions to develop alignment in your company:

Define the culture in your company:

_____

_____

_____

_____

_____

Is culture aligned at all levels in the company?

_____

_____

If "yes," what did you do to get this done?

_____

_____

If "no," what do you need to do to get this done?

_____

_____

If "no," how long will it realistically take to get this done?

_____

_____

If "no," who in the organization needs to be involved?

_____

_____

Define a key strategic initiative in your company:

_____

_____

_____

_____

_____

Is the strategic objective "aligned" throughout the entire organiza-tion, meaning does everyone in the company know how he or she directly or indirectly supports this goal?

_____

_____

If "yes," what did you do to get this done?

_____

_____

If "no," what do you need to do to get this done?

_____

_____

If "no," how long will it realistically take to get this done?

_____

_____

If "no," who in the organization needs to be involved?

_____

_____

Is culture aligned with strategic objective throughout the organization?

_____

_____

_____

If "yes," what did you do to get this done?

_____

_____

_____

If "no," what do you need to do to get this done?

_____

_____

_____

If "no," how long will it realistically take to get this done?

_____

_____

_____

_____

If "no," who in the organization needs to be involved?

_____

_____

_____

_____

Define a tactical step supporting a key strategic initiative in your company.

_____

_____

_____

_____

Is the tactical step aligned with the key strategic objective throughout the entire organization—meaning does everyone in the company know what he or she is supposed to do in support of the tactical step?

_____

_____

If "yes," what did you do to get this done?

_____

_____

If "no," what do you need to do to get this done?

_____

_____

If "no," how long will it realistically take to get this done?

_____

_____

If "no," who in the organization needs to be involved?

_____

_____

Is culture aligned with this tactical step throughout the organization?

_____

_____

_____

If "yes," what did you do to get this done?

_____

_____

_____

If "no," what do you need to do to get this done?

_____

_____

_____

If "no," how long will it realistically take to get this done?

_____

_____

_____

_____

If "no," who in the organization needs to be involved?

_____

_____

_____

_____

In the absence of clearly defined goals, we become strangely loyal to performing daily acts of trivia.

— Author Unknown

SCORING THE GAME

If you have built organizational alignment, congratulations! You have scored a GRAND SLAM home run—four runs for your team! This is huge—very well done!

If you have not built organizational alignment, start writing good speeches for after the game and rethink your practice goals. You'll have a group of unhappy players who need to work toward becoming a team.

6th INNING SCORECARD

What are your key takeaways from this inning?

_____

_____

_____

_____

_____

_____

_____

_____

_____

_____

_____

_____

_____

_____

_____

_____

_____

_____

Major League Profile – Walt Disney

Walt Disney created several businesses that were aligned with one another. Success from one company helped leverage success in the others.

In the 1920s, Disney created Mickey Mouse, the cartoon character that has permeated almost every country and culture in the world. He is also the co-founder of Walt Disney Productions, which created such animated films as *Snow White and the Seven Dwarfs*, *Fantasia*, and *Dumbo*. In 1955, Disney created and opened Disneyland in Anaheim, California, considered by many to be the "gold standard" for theme parks in the world.

Disney was the inaugural recipient of a star on the Anaheim Walk of Stars, was posthumously awarded a Congressional Gold Medal in 1968, and also had a minor planet, 4017 Disneya, named after him.

Disney offered two leadership lessons:

1. **Never stop dreaming:** As a leader, you must never stop envisioning possibilities and stop innovating. The possibilities are limited only by your imagination. If you want to build something of significance, constantly be thinking about more creative ways to achieve your vision. Never underestimate the power of your imagination to stand out from the rest of the crowd.

   Disney was a dreamer. He never stopped trying new things, creating new cartoons, regardless of his level of success.

2. **Never give up:** Be persistent. As a leader, you must have the tenacity to persevere. Everyone goes through tough times, especially when chasing a huge dream or goal. It is your tenacity that separates you from the rest and attracts others to follow you.

Disney suffered many setbacks throughout his long career. He was in business for ten years before having success with the creation of Mickey Mouse.

PART 3

....

The Late Innings

Playing to Win Consistently

7th INNING

Investing In and Protecting Your Assets—Baseball

CULTURE

Developing and protecting a strong culture for your youth baseball program is imperative if you want to build a sustainable program supportive of your mission (see 1st inning—Definition of Success).

Below is a summary of two cultures. Take a moment and think about the differences:

Player-Driven Culture

- **Why:** To provide an environment where kids are having fun while learning how to compete in a loving and supportive environment that teaches baseball and life skills.

- **How:** Coaches are inspirational leaders who enjoy teaching the game, working with individual skills, and motivating others in pursuit of building successful teams. The baseball program operates at a very high level with every player having a remarkable experience.

- **Outcome:** As a result, kids learn baseball skills and valuable life lessons about hard work, discipline, leadership, and teamwork.

The All-Star team does well in post-season tournament play—year after year. A strong baseball community is also developed and maintained.

Winning-Driven Culture

- **Why:** The All-Star team does well in post-season tournament play—year after year.

- **How:** Coaches lead by intimidation and coercion.

- **Outcome:** Kids feel pressure to perform at the risk of being castigated. The top players are developed and rewarded while second-tier players are neglected or even abused.

Let's just assume that you believe the Player-Driven Culture is preferred. In this environment, a winning program becomes the outcome when players are the focus.

A danger exists when the focus shifts to a Winning-Driven Culture, where winning takes priority over creating a remarkable experience for the kids. What invariably happens is that players and their experiences become secondary to what is now the primary objective of winning at all costs.

Take a look at your local Little League, or ask friends in other communities to share anecdotes about the type of cultures they are experiencing. Don't ask coaches, unless you are talking to coaches in other leagues. Asking a coach to look in the mirror doesn't lend itself to complete objectivity. Remember, your brand is what other people say about you. If you want to build a strong culture, recognize that it takes purposeful intent and time.

During the 3rd inning, we spent some time defining the importance of culture. Identifying the values and ways in which a baseball program will conduct itself and be known is the beginning of developing a culture that is valuable. Practically speaking, the second step is to get buy-in from the board of directors, league administrators, and coaches. Without this buy-in, you can't move ahead to the third step—putting it into action. The fourth step is integration, which means the program takes best practices and rolls them out among all teams and divisions. The fifth, final, and most important step to institutionalize this culture, which develops into a long-term asset, will sustain itself over time.

Culture is what shows up on the baseball diamond. It is not a policy, procedure, and directive. It is what players experience and what coaches project.

FIELDS

Imagine showing up for Opening Day of the baseball season. The weather this day is sunny and warm, but the fields haven't yet recovered from yesterday's rainfall. Every ball field is a mud pit, with poor drainage and soaking wet grass, which leaves no protection for the players and coaches.

Three years ago, the city where I live invested nearly $1 million to improve field conditions, which included improved drainage, artificial turf, a covered batting cage, covered dugouts, and a concession stand. This investment will produce dramatically improved outcomes for the player experience—for many years to come.

Players, parents, coaches, and the community are thrilled to have a true asset, which results in having ball fields that are actually playable, substantially increasing the number of games that can be played each season.

Take a moment and think about your office space, manufacturing facility, or warehouse. Have you invested in and adequately protected the value of these tangible assets to maximize the potential for sustaining your business in a profitable way?

BOARD

Organizations are run by people, and youth baseball programs are usually run by a volunteer group of parents. My #1 piece of advice is to ensure that the volunteer Board of Directors focuses on the Little League's desired outcomes—taking on its responsibility of keeping the culture intact and delivering on its mission—or definition of success.

MANAGERS/COACHES

In my opinion, leader development can never be too big of an investment. In baseball, the leaders are the team manager and coaches—the creators of culture. The leaders who show up at the ball field to coach, instruct, and mold young players create that team's culture. How do they inspire, lead, motivate, and teach the kids? How do they help parents become supportive fans? How do they conduct themselves during the game with umpires, their team, and the opposing coaches and players?

This stuff shows up all the time, whether at team practice, a Little League game, or an All Star tournament. Usually, poor managers and coaches make for poor business leaders. They exhibit one or more of the following characteristics:

1. They intimidate and badger—whether it be kids, other coaches, umpires, or parents.

2. They are unorganized and without plan or purpose.

3. They do not inspire followership.

If any of the three characteristics above show up in your league, ask yourself, "What is the cost of this dysfunction to the leagues, teams, and players? What is the damage being done, and how long am I willing to let this situation continue?"

Bad managers and coaches can become good. Good managers and coaches can become great. Invest the time to recognize what is wrong—then fix it! Stop doing what doesn't work and commit to positive change.

PLAYERS

Bad youth baseball coaches think of players as assets—cogs in a machine whose sole purpose is to help the coach win games. That is NOT what I'm talking about here.

Think of players as ambassadors for your program. What do you want them to say to their friends and parents about their experiences as players on your team, or participants in a league? The manifestation of a strong league is a very high percentage of players RAVING about their experiences playing youth baseball. How does that show up on the field? Below are some ideas:

1. Fun environment—after all—this is a game!

2. Failure is encouraged, as part of the learning process.

3. Hard work, effort, discipline, and commitment to team are emphasized.

4. Winning games is a by-product of team and player development—not the sole objective to please a coach.

BRAND

The brand of a youth baseball program is essentially what others say about your program. One thing I've learned over the years is that people talk, whether it is flattering or unflattering. Be mindful of what you want others to say—and work toward that!

Little League Profile - Maddie Bradshaw

Protecting her businesses assets is one thing Maddie Bradshaw has done to build a thriving company.

Maddie is the president, founder, and head designer of M3 Girl Designs LLC. She is currently sixteen years old and started her business at age ten. With $300 of her own money and a unique idea, Snap Caps® bottle cap necklaces was born and now her necklaces are a "must have" accessory for tween girls. To date, the company has generated over $5 million in sales.

The company took huge steps toward becoming a growing and sustainable company after an appearance on the TV show *Shark Tank,* which aired in February 2012. Maddie, her twelve-year-old sister Margot, and her mother asked the "sharks"—a panel of five investors—to invest $300,000 in exchange for a 15 percent stake in the company. That equates to a company worth $2 million—not bad for a young teenager. Maddie ended up negotiating a partnership deal with three of the sharks, which included the $300,000 to expand the business, but more importantly, ongoing mentoring from guest shark Lori Greiner, a well-known QVC television personality and inventor of more than 350 products.

Maddie has received a crash course in everything from trademarks and LLCs (Limited Liability Companies) to marketing and human resources. Her mother acts as the company CEO, helping to make business and financial decisions and serving as an adult when consent is needed to sign deals. Maddie sees the importance in marketing, noting that her products are now sold in more than 6,000 U.S. retail outlets, including Amazon.com and Nordstrom.

As for the secrets to her success, Maddie truly believes that, "You have to love what you do. I took my love for art, created an idea, and ran with it." Maddie admits that she has outgrown Snap Caps; she is not worried about the company becoming a one-hit wonder. While her sister Margot, age twelve, has become more involved with the direction and design of Snap Caps, Maddie has added a new Spark of Life line of necklaces and stackable bracelets targeted to her age group. She believes the company will continue to evolve and grow as she continues to mature and become an adult, explaining that "As my tastes change, so will the products."

Investing In and Protecting Your Assets—Business

OVERVIEW

If asked "What are the assets in your company?" how many of you would say something like, "my intellectual property, property, plant and equipment, customer base, and value of the brand"? If so, give yourself partial credit for a good answer.

If you didn't think of a strong company culture and your people as among the most valuable assets in your company, try thinking about how well the business would do tomorrow if you were the only person who showed up to work? If that is not a pretty picture.... I think you get the idea.

The 7th inning in the game of building value in your business is all about developing and protecting your assets, from a variety of perspectives. My expectation is that by this chapter's end, you will recognize the value and importance of company culture and retaining good employees. The next steps involve implementing ideas that can enhance the value they bring to your organization.

CULTURE

A vibrant culture binds a company together. It creates an environment that enables strong leaders and teams to be developed. This environment improves the likelihood that business strategy and tactical plans get executed. Strong culture tends to result in low employee turnover.

173

A by-product of a bad company culture is high employee turnover. It has been said, and I believe it to be true, that the cost of employee turnover (when you lose an employee you don't want to lose) can be quantified at 150 percent of that person's compensation. Think of the loss of institutional knowledge, team chemistry, recruiting and hiring expense, onboarding, and the time it takes to bring a new employee through the learning curve of getting him to where the former employee functioned. Wouldn't you rather strive for low employee turnover?

As an example of low turnover, let's talk about one of my favorite companies. Costco has 200,000 employees and 5 percent employee turnover for those who stay a year or more. That means employees stay with the company on average for twenty years. Employees like working at Costco and don't leave for greener pastures. It just so happens that leaders at Costco say, "Culture is the *only* thing that led to the success of our company." Do you think they're onto something? Let's run the numbers:

Many companies have a 20 percent turnover rate and think that is a good outcome. Costco's employee turnover rate is 5 percent per year. The difference in turnover rate is 15 percent, or 30,000 employees per year. Costco doesn't have to rehire and train because its vibrant culture keeps employees passionate and engaged. What is this impact on profitability and the bottom line? Assuming the average compensation is $50,000 per employee, the benefit of a strong company culture is $1.5 billion dollars. In August 2012, Costco was valued at twenty-seven times its annual earnings. Using my example above, you could conclude that a strong culture and low employee turnover translate to over $40 billion in company value. That's a big number. Do I have your attention yet?

BOARD

Many great resources out there describe how a strong Board of Directors should function. For this book's purposes, I'll list two key things I believe are important, based on what I've seen during my professional career:

1. Make sure the right C level leaders (CEO, CFO, COO, and CTO) are in place.

2. Make sure these leaders are institutionalizing a strong and vibrant culture.

LEADERSHIP

Assuming you have the right leaders in place, my advice is to invest, invest, and then invest some more in developing strong leadership capabilities. Executive coaching, building a strong and vibrant culture, and enhancing team-building capabilities are three areas I believe are important to get right—*before* focusing on things like strategic and tactical plan development. Putting strategy and tactics before culture, leaders, and teams is like putting the cart before the horse. It just doesn't work.

EMPLOYEES ARE NOT CREATED EQUAL

Employees are not created equal. If you had a service company with 100 employees and the company was valued at $50 million, then on average, each employee has produced $.5 million of value.

Let's identify groups of employees that produce higher value:

1. Executives who truly lead, inspire, motivate, and create the environment for a vibrant organization.

2. Revenue producers who go out of their way to build sustainable relationships and increasingly profitable business to the company.

3. Up-and-coming talent. These are the highly engaged individuals who can grow into future executives and managers.

These groups of employees usually represent about 30 percent of the total workforce.

My question is: What are you doing to develop and retain individuals in this group? Losing employees in this category will destroy value in your company.

Let's identify a second group of employees who do their jobs adequately:

1. Executives who are competent at their jobs but are actually biding time.

2. Revenue producers who seem content with the status quo. Customers they bring to the company come and go, but no significant profitable growth comes out of these efforts.

3. Employees who do their jobs but never try to transform the ordinary into extraordinary.

These employees usually represent about 50 percent of the total workforce.

My questions are: What are you doing to move these employees into the 1st category? What is the cost of maintaining the status-quo with this group? How much company value can you create by moving a percentage of these employees into the top tier group?

The third group of employees looks like this:

1. Executives who are actually damaging the company culture and are ineffective leaders.

2. Revenue producers who do not build healthy relationships with customers. They don't care whether new business is profitable or unprofitable.

3. Employees who dislike their jobs and co-workers, but stay because they want a paycheck. These employees actively destroy work teams and chip away at the company culture.

My experience is that about 20 percent of employees fall into this third group.

My question is: What are you doing to move these employees up to second-tier employees, assuming that is possible. If it is not possible, why haven't you invited these employees to be successful somewhere else and turned them into former employees? The cost of not removing them is actually destroying value in your company.

CUSTOMERS ARE NOT CREATED EQUAL

Just as all employees are not created equal, it is also true that not all customers are created equal—some provide more revenue than others.

So let me start by asking a question: To double your company's profitability, do you have to double its revenue? The answer is: Absolutely not—and the math behind application of the Pareto principle may astound you!

The Pareto principle asserts that 80 percent of results come from 20 percent of effort. In business, this generally applies to revenue and profits. Most leaders focus on the 20 percent of customers who drive

80 percent of revenue. Instead, why not focus on the 20 percent of customers who drive 80 percent of profit?

Below is an extreme but real life example—this stuff happens!

1. Company has $40 million in annual revenue and $4 million in operating profit.

2. Company has assumption that in order to increase operating profit to $8 million, it is necessary to generate $80 million in revenue.

By peeling back the onion, here's what was really going on inside the company:

1. Division A: generated 80 percent of revenue—$32 million produced break-even results.

2. Division B: generated 20 percent of revenue—$8 million produced $4 million in operating profit.

So, to double operating profit, one way to get there would be to invest in initiatives to double the size of Division B, increasing total company revenue by 20 percent. This plan requires far fewer people, less space requirements, and less investment capital than going down the path of doubling the size of the entire company and investing in a non-profitable division.

Therefore, with all things being equal:

1. Company now has $48 million in annual revenue, an increase of 20 percent.

2. Company now has $8 million in operating profit, an increase of 100 percent.

3. Division A still has $32 million in revenue with break-even results.

4. Division B now has $16 million in revenue with $8 million in operating profit.

Yes, this is a very simplified example, and another approach would have been to optimize Division A. Having said that, are you missing the obvious in your company? Are you making decisions about office space, staffing, investment capital needed, or acquisition strategy, based on general information or a detailed understanding of what drives profitability in your company? My advice is to make sure you truly understand the answers to these questions before making long-term strategic business decisions.

BUILDING AND EQUIPMENT

What do customers experience when they visit your offices? What do employees experience when they show up to work? Are the facilities clean and well-maintained? Are they run-down and near the end of their useful life? There is both functionality and perception, and both are important.

I know of a CEO who wants to shift his company's direction from a manufacturing driven revenue model to a sales and marketing driven model. The building exterior is unkempt. The interior is several decades old. While comfortable to the CEO, the image his building projects is that of a company on its last legs, not exactly the image he wants to portray. To develop and protect his business, it makes sense for him to invest in appearances. Image is important and people pay attention.

INTELLECTUAL PROPERTY

My father-in-law is a smart and dynamic guy. An aeronautical engineer by training, he eventually became a high level executive at The Boeing Company, and after retiring, later became mayor of a small but very well-known resort community. Outside of work at The Boeing Company and during his professional career, he had a business partner who invented a medical device that thirty-five years later still dominates market share. The product is the Ballard Trach Care Closed Suction System.

In the beginning, the inventor secured patent protection and the intellectual property rights to the invention. Securing patent protection turned out to be a big deal.

During the early years, my father-in-law and his business partner rented a warehouse and developed a company culture while selling and making the product. Growing the company in a profitable way was tough, but some labor was cheap. I know because my wife was a teenager at the time and helped on the production line cutting plastic tubing with an X-Acto knife. (She didn't know about child exploitation laws at the time, but she came away unscathed.) Being mission-driven, my father-in-law and his business partner wanted to share this invention with the health care community, knowing their product dramatically improved the way lung fluids were drained. Doing it by building a business was tough—there had to be a better way!

To make a long story short, they eventually shut down the business but licensed the rights to produce and sell this invention to a company called Ballard Medical Devices (years later it was sold to Kimberly Clark). Over thirty-five years later, the inventor is still being well-compensated for improving patients' lives. Royalty income replaced salary and bonus. Business risk was transformed into financial reward. In this case, the intellectual property became the most important asset developed.

In your business, have you created something unique and special? Do you have trademark protection for unique trade names? Is your written material copyrighted? Are your inventions protected by patent? Are you locking down your trade secrets? Take the time to determine whether you have any intangible assets (things you cannot touch and feel) that you wouldn't want someone else to steal. Don't try to copyright or patent on your own; seek the advice of an attorney who specializes in these matters.

Okay. Now it is time to continue writing in your game plan journal and to answer the following questions to identify and protect important assets in your company:

What are your company's most important assets? List them below:

_____

_____

_____

_____

_____

_____

_____

_____

_____

_____

_____

_____

_____

_____

_____

_____

_____

_____

_____

What are you doing to develop and protect your most important assets?

_____

_____

_____

_____

_____

_____

_____

_____

_____

_____

_____

_____

_____

_____

_____

_____

_____

_____

_____

_____

_____

What are you doing to eliminate the non-performing assets in your company?

_____

_____

_____

_____

_____

_____

_____

_____

_____

_____

_____

_____

_____

_____

_____

_____

_____

_____

How much time will you invest to develop and protect your most important assets?

_____

_____

_____

_____

_____

_____

_____

_____

_____

How will you know whether you are successful or unsuccessful?

_____

_____

_____

_____

_____

_____

_____

_____

_____

Not taking the time to identify and categorize all of your tangible and in-tangible assets is akin to not knowing the position each ball player should play on your team—or if he should be on the team!

Invest the time to figure this out—or don't do this at your peril—the choice is yours.

— Earl Bell

SCORING THE GAME

If you have identified your key assets and have an executable plan in place to develop, protect, and retain your assets, then congratulations are in order. You have set up your company for repeatable success.

If you have not done so, your company is at risk for a bad year or years in the future.

7th INNING SCORECARD

What are your key takeaways from this inning?

_____

_____

_____

_____

_____

_____

_____

_____

_____

_____

_____

_____

_____

_____

_____

_____

_____

_____

_____

Major League Profile – Bill Gates

Protecting business assets is what enabled Bill Gates to build Microsoft into a multi-billion dollar company.

Gates co-founded Microsoft with Paul Allen. When approached by IBM to develop an operating system for their personal computers, Gates and Allen created the MS-DOS program and retained the intellectual property rights for MS-DOS through copyright protection. This pivotal event launched Microsoft to stratospheric success and the rest is history.

Now the second richest man in the world, Gates is active in philanthropic work at the Bill and Melinda Gates Foundation and has given over $28 billion to their causes.

Gates offers three leadership lessons:

1. **Nothing comes easy**: It takes years of dedicated work to achieve mastery. If you want to see success in your life, don't look for an easy path or short-cuts.

2. **Follow your passion:** If you are not passionate about your work, you will eventually lose interest and focus, which ultimately sets you up for failure. Money will follow passion.

   Gates was passionate about computer programming and found the work to be interesting, which motivated him to do more. This self-training is what gave him the experience to start Microsoft.

3. **Give back to your community:** It is a reflection of your character. Are you a giver and blessing to the community, or are you a taker who expects the community to bless you. Givers become people of significance who are remembered through time for making a difference in the world. People don't follow you because you take from them; they follow you because you give to them. To be successful in life, strive to give more than you take from society.

8th INNING

Dealing With Risk—Baseball

This inning is all about playing defense while preventing and/or preparing for bad situations. An easy way to think about risk is that it represents the potential for an activity or action, or inactivity or inaction, leading to a bad outcome. Ways to confront risks associated with bad outcomes can be divided into five categories:

1. Prevent risk

2. Manage risk

3. Insure risk

4. Ignore risk

5. Crisis management

How baseball leaders choose to manage or ignore this risk can mean the difference between a thriving program and one that figuratively *dies on the vine.*

PREVENT RISK

So here's a quick tip to accelerate a plan to prevent bad things from happening. Take a look at what successful baseball programs do—and copy them. Another thing you can do is observe how the horrible baseball programs operate and use them as a model for what NOT to do. Pretty simple, isn't it?

As an example, let's talk about arm injuries—probably the most prevalent events that hamper young baseball pitchers. Mercer Island's pitchers were certainly no exception until one of the coaches in our youth select baseball program learned about a dynamic arm conditioning program that the University of Washington baseball program put in place for its entire pitching staff. As a result, this program's pitching staff has had ZERO arm injuries for the past seven years. Hmm...that seemed like a good thing to copy, so we did.

Preventative actions are designed to mitigate the likelihood of bad outcomes. I'll provide a few more examples:

1. Do background checks on all managers and coaches to prevent those with criminal backgrounds from working with young athletes.

2. Establish a code of conduct so managers, coaches, players, and parents all understand expected behaviors.

3. Teach and model positive behavior so arguments don't occur at games, and if an argument does happen, it doesn't lead to a fight.

4. Teach each player how to avoid serious injury on the playing field from such events as getting hit by a pitch thrown at his head.

MANAGE RISK

If bad things happen, how will you respond, and will you be adequately prepared? Preparation is really what managing risk is all about.

Contingent actions are designed to mitigate bad outcomes. I'll provide a few examples:

1. A first aid kit and plenty of ice packs are available for tending to minor injuries.

2. A phone list of all players and parents is kept and used if parents don't show up at the end of practice to pick up their young athletes.

3. If a parent or player becomes unruly at a game, the manager and coach know exactly how to respond because they have a preplanned course of action.

INSURE RISK

When the likelihood is low that a bad event will happen, but the seriousness of this potential bad event could lead to a big financial burden, then insuring risk is the appropriate way to go.

Liability insurance policies are designed to mitigate these events. Below are a few examples:

1. A significant injury requires hospitalization.

2. A player or spectator gets hurt and decides to sue the league for personal injury.

3. Ball fields suffer total loss due to fire or vandalism.

IGNORE RISK

The ostrich strategy can also be implemented. It happens when risks are identified but leaders choose not to prevent, manage, nor insure against these risks. Many times, it works just fine…that is until something bad happens!

CRISIS MANAGEMENT

In a crisis, the unimaginable has happened. You may have put in place the best plans to prevent, manage, and insure risk. Sometimes, it just doesn't matter.

Dan Weedin is an expert in crisis management. He likes to say, *"We all know that being prepared for crisis is critical to surviving one. Whether it's a natural disaster, an economic crisis, or a travesty like what happened at Penn State University, you must be ready to make tough and smart decisions."*

He also asserts that *"part of your crisis management process needs to define how to protect your brand and reputation. Reputation risk may be just as damaging as the crisis that started it. Just ask BP [British Petroleum]! You must have a plan in place to communicate effectively to employees, investors, regulators, clients, prospective customers, the media, and your community. Failure to do this will lead to distrust, loss of reputation, and lost revenue. Having a plan in place, on the other hand, will set you in a position to not only protect your good name, but take advantage of the opportunity to thrive."*

A well-designed and practiced crisis response plan is needed to manage the unimaginable. Below are a few examples of what can literally cripple a program.

1. Bad behavior: A manager or coach molests a player.

2. Bad press: An out-of-control parent engages in a fight with an umpire, another parent, or even player.

3. Bad governance: Little League funds are embezzled and trust is breached. No insurance was in place for risk of embezzlement.

Crisis management proactively defines the solution to "once in a life-time events." These events happen—trust me! You are far better off developing this action plan *before* the crisis hits your company. You will add significant value to your business by being prepared for the unimaginable.

WHAT TO DO ABOUT RISK?

To protect your program and ensure it continues to thrive and grow, invest the time to identify everything that can go wrong, and then place each topic or item in one of the following categories:

1. Prevent risk

2. Manage risk

3. Insure risk

4. Ignore risk

5. Crisis management

Preventing risk requires *proactive* action to make sure the negative out-come doesn't happen.

Managing risk is *reactive* in nature, and it is all about implementing contingent behaviors in response to bad things happening.

Insuring risk is a financial instrument in which you pay a small amount of money (an insurance premium) against bad things happening that will pay off big if they do happen.

Ignoring risk is a choice—people do it all the time. It works until bad things happen; then, no mechanism or plan is in place to deal with the bad outcome.

Crisis management is all about managing the unimaginable. If the unimaginable were to happen, would you prefer to know in advance how you would respond? Chances are, a proactive level of preparedness as opposed to a reactive response to chaos will mean the difference between survival and your program's extinction.

Little League Profile – Adam Horwitz

Dealing with risk by moving forward on business ventures that were low risk and high reward has been Adam Horwitz's focus in pursuit of his entrepreneurial dreams.

Four years ago at age fifteen, Adam had one goal: to create a million-dollar company before he turned twenty-one. His businesses did not require significant start-up capital.

Four years and thirty unsuccessful, self-funded, web-based companies later, Adam launched Mobile Monopoly, an online course that teaches people how to earn money by generating mobile marketing leads. This venture earned Adam a six-figure profit.

In addition to Mobile Monopoly, Adam added several other online courses, each earning him six figures or more. Adam did break his million-dollar-revenue goal before his eighteenth birthday. The company he founded, Local Mobile Monopoly, is a multimedia training platform designed to help business owners.

What drives Adam is his love for building a business and watching it grow into something big. According to Adam, "The journey is the most exciting part."

Adam's latest venture is called YepText, a text messaging service that sends ads and promotions to a customer's smart phone. Unlike other text messaging services that are more complicated and targeted toward the Fortune 500 list, YepText is specifically targeted to the small business niche.

Adam's message to other aspiring entrepreneurs: "Anything is possible now; just make sure that you take action and never, ever give up."

Dealing with Risk—Business

Okay. Let's now spend some time taking what you just read about the five ways to address risk and use that model to categorize and develop possible action plans for twenty types of risk.

PREVENT RISK

1. **Too much business growth:** Develop a "Just say no" policy when the decision to accept new customers or business would put your company at risk of imploding. Remember that not all new business is good business. Refusal of business would assume that you've already determined that all of your existing business is comprised of good customers who are producing acceptable profit margin.

2. **Losing key customers:** What are you doing to ensure that for your profitable customers (again I assume you know who they are), the customer experience is moving from ordinary to extraordinary? The goal should be to WOW your customers so they cannot imagine doing business with one of your competitors.

3. **Embezzlement:** Sound financial internal controls can prevent embezzlement. Engage the professional help from your Controller, if he is a CPA, or bring in an accounting firm to help set up effective internal controls over your assets—cash, receivables, payables, inventory, and equipment. The cost of not taking this preventative action can put you out of business if a smart enough thief ends up working for you in the accounting department.

4. **Hiring practices:** There are legal and illegal hiring practices. Do you know what they are? If not, engage the help of experienced

Human Resources professionals who will keep you out of the courtroom.

5. **Theft:** Preventing theft would be a proactive measure. Banks use video cameras as a preventative deterrent.

6. **Loss in productivity:** Lost productivity often happens when employee morale declines and workers lose passion for their work. What are you doing to ensure productivity loss doesn't happen?

7. **Company culture gone bad:** Companies periodically lose their way and healthy culture becomes toxic. Think of company culture as the most important asset not on the balance sheet. Strong culture is institutionalized. It survives up and down cycles and changes in leadership and teams.

MANAGE RISK

1. **Insufficient cash flow from business to pay bills**: I assume your Chief Financial Officer is capable of ensuring working capital is properly managed and that appropriate forms of debt and equity financing are in place to support investment, growth, and operations.

2. **Customer concentration:** What will you do when one customer becomes a significant part of your business? Locally, here in Washington State, many companies do work for Microsoft, but whoever the large customer is you depend on, remember that its business could come and go quickly. A couple of suggestions would be to determine whether the small profit margin that companies typically get working for Microsoft or a similar company as a supplier/provider is worth the effort. If the answer is "yes," then moving your cost structure to variable instead of fixed for expenses associated with serving such a customer is one way to

manage this risk, so if the revenues suddenly go away, so will the associated expenses.

3. **Supplier concentration:** You should NEVER place all of your eggs in one basket; this wisdom especially applies to key suppliers. Develop partnerships with at least two and preferably three vendors for each key component.

4. **Toxic employees:** Every now and then, the hiring process will not filter out employees who turn out to be toxic. I suggest engaging experienced Human Resources professionals who know how effectively and legally to protect the company's best interests while removing toxic employees from the workplace.

INSURE RISK

1. **Errors and omissions:** Enlist consulting advice from an experienced insurance consultant for professional services companies.

2. **Fire:** Enlist assistance from a property & casualty insurance agent or consultant.

3. **Auto accident:** Enlist assistance from an auto insurance agent or consultant.

4. **Business interruption:** Let's say a fire burns your business to the ground. You may have fire insurance to rebuild the premises, but how will you recover from lost revenues and profits while the business furiously works to reopen its doors? Business interruption insurance covers this risk.

5. **Health insurance:** Health care costs will continue to rise significantly and become an even larger component of company cost structures. Hire a reputable employee benefits consultant to

navigate this increasingly complex world. Retaining employees is a business risk, and attractive employee benefit plans do help retain employees. The rules for health coverage compliance are also getting more complex, and penalties for non-compliance are getting bigger, not smaller.

6. **Litigation from a former employee:** This situation happens all the time, especially if the culture is toxic. A disgruntled former employee may rightly or wrongly sue the company and its owners and managers.

IGNORE RISK

1. **Violent crime:** You're probably scratching your head and asking "Why did Earl choose to ignore the risk of violent crime in the workplace?" The question I'll toss back is, "What do companies currently do to prevent or manage the risk of violent crime?" I'll suggest that most companies do nothing because they view the risk as being extremely small. Do you look at this risk the same way? If not, what will you do to prevent or manage this risk?

CRISIS MANAGEMENT

1. **Bad press:** Imagine waking up in the morning to discover that your company is the headline story—in an unflattering way. Imagine being the President of Penn State University and discovering that a former coach on your football staff is a child molester! Do you think the leaders at Penn State proactively knew how they would manage this crisis? I suspect that its lack of a plan will cost the university irreparable harm and financial hardship beyond comprehension. My suggestion is to engage crisis management professionals who will take your leadership team through corporate war games simulation—so when bad things

unexpectedly happen, you and your team are ready and able to respond effectively.

2. **Product malfunction:** Quality control procedures are intended as a way to prevent risk. However, what happens when they don't work? What if you were a brake manufacturer and had as a potential risk that your product led to a freeway death? Do you have a plan in place to respond to this "once in a lifetime" event that seems to happen more than once in a lifetime? If not, why not? If you are choosing to ignore a potential crisis, understand the potential risk that is being taken on.

3. **Production shutdown:** Unions periodically go on strike and production can get shut down. How will you respond? Are you taking proactive steps to prevent this risk from happening, or do you find yourself in a precarious situation every four years?

Let's review some key points before I give you a practice drill to work on.

1. Five ways exist to deal with risk. Ignoring risk is one option.

2. Invest the time to identify each type of risk present in your business and determine how you will respond to each.

3. Proactively identifying and responding to risk will keep your company in the game and significantly improve the likelihood of remaining a viable entity after bad things happen.

Okay. Now it is time to continue writing in your game plan journal and to answer the following questions to develop a plan to address and respond to business risks:

Identify ways your company could be at risk that you will prevent through proactive behaviors. For each risk, identify the proactive behavior and develop a brief action plan.

Identify ways your company could be at risk that you will manage through contingent behaviors. For each risk, identify the contingent behavior and develop a brief action plan.

_____

_____

_____

_____

_____

_____

_____

_____

_____

_____

_____

_____

_____

_____

_____

_____

_____

_____

_____

_____

Identify ways your company could be at risk that you will protect by insuring the risk. For each risk, identify the event that triggers insurance coverage.

Bonus tip: Hire a business insurance consultant you trust to assist in this exercise.

_____

_____

_____

_____

_____

_____

_____

_____

_____

_____

_____

_____

_____

_____

_____

_____

_____

_____

Identify risks you will ignore. For each risk, develop a model that quantifies the potential likelihood of the bad event occurring, along with the negative impact to your business.

Identify ways your company could be crippled, and invest the time to get your team engaged in developing a comprehensive crisis management plan in response to each catastrophic event.

_____

_____

_____

_____

_____

_____

_____

_____

_____

_____

_____

_____

_____

_____

_____

_____

_____

_____

Risk is a function of how poorly a strategy will perform if the "wrong" scenario occurs!

— Michael Porter, Professor, Harvard University

SCORING THE GAME

If you have identified the things that can go wrong in your business and determined an appropriate way to manage each risk, then you are well-positioned to ensure your company will stay in business and not be negatively harmed when bad things happen!

If that is the case, your opponent did not score any runs this inning. In the games of both business and baseball, playing good defense is necessary to ensure sustainable winning.

8th INNING SCORECARD

What are your key takeaways from this inning?

Major League Profile – Donald Trump

Dealing with risk is something Donald Trump has done throughout his entire business career. As a real-estate developer and television personality, he is the Chairman of the Trump Organization and has accumulated over $2.7 billion in net wealth.

Donald Trump's father was a successful real estate developer named Fred Trump. After graduating from a Military Academy, Donald Trump decided to follow in his father's footsteps in the real estate business.

Several successes early in his career were wiped out in 1989 when an economic recession led to Trump declaring bankruptcy. The company balance sheet was over-leveraged with too much debt, primarily to finance casino investments using junk bonds. After negotiating deals with his creditors that included a repayment plan, most of this debt was repaid by 1994.

Starting in 1997, Trump started his business comeback and has since developed several large scale real estate projects in many cities. His visibility became even greater as a television personality when becoming host of the TV show *The Apprentice.*

Trump offers three leadership lessons:

1. **Think big:** A great leader needs to see things that others cannot see. Trump believed in making big bets and huge investments in real estate because he saw potential. His ability to be nimble while thinking big resulted in making a strong comeback after declaring bankruptcy in the 1980s.

2. **Have great energy:** Energy drives passion and passion transforms the impossible into the possible.

3. **Be resilient:** Self-belief and tenacity resulted in Trump coming out of bankruptcy and rallying to great success. Failure is part of a normal business cycle. The important thing is not to think about how to avoid failure, but instead, to find ways to bounce back after experiencing setbacks.

9th INNING
Systematizing Process—Baseball

Have you ever noticed how some Little League programs continually produce strong All Star teams *and* a great experience for the kids while other Little Leagues may sporadically have *either* a strong All Star team or an overall great experience for the kids, and a third group does neither? Here's my assessment of why these scenarios happen:

1. Consistently strong programs have systematized what works. Culture is healthy and sustained. Player and team development best practices are documented, teachable, repeatable, and institutionalized.

2. Sporadically strong programs periodically have great leaders and coaches. Either a healthy league culture is not developed and sustained or the year-long Little League experience is not systematized.

3. Poorly run programs have neither developed nor institutionalized healthy culture, nor implemented systematized best practices.

During the 3rd inning, we spent time talking about Culture. During the 9th inning, let's talk about what systematizing process looks like.

I'll begin by saying, "Every system works *exactly* as it is designed to work!" Poorly run programs are designed to work that way. Malfunction and dysfunction are allowed to happen, and horrible outcomes are the result. Conversely, a *well-oiled machine* is that way for a reason; it was designed to be that way.

I'd like to share briefly my progression as a baseball coach, and then offer some lessons learned over six years about how systematizing process leads to development of strong teams:

YEAR 1

Coaching six-year-old boys playing T-ball was an adventure. I came on as an assistant coach to help a very nice man who realized that one dad trying to corral twelve precocious boys was a bigger challenge than any one person could handle. Tom recruited three dads to help, including me. Below is a quick recap of the season:

1. We had no real plan for the season other than to show up and make T-ball fun for the boys.

2. Hitting practice consisted of eleven boys watching the twelfth try to hit a ball off the tee.

3. Throwing and catching practice involved lots of throwing, but not a lot of catching.

4. Victory was getting runners to go to the right bases.

5. The biggest challenge as a coach was to be more interesting than the daisies constantly being picked on the ball field grass. The final score: Daisies, seven players—Coaches, five players.

6. Some players wanted to be there—others didn't. See score above!

7. Games consisted of everyone batting with no score being kept.

8. Biggest lessons learned: We didn't know what we were doing—and these boys had a one-minute attention span! After the two-minute mark, all sense of order was lost and chaos took over.

If you are running a business where chaos is the culture, purpose and direction is lacking, and there is no foresight into how to develop your employees, departments, or company, then you probably see similarities between your company and my experience with this group of players. In both instances, many opportunities to improve can be found! On a scale of 1 to 10, the level of systematized processes was as low as you could get—or in other words—a solid 1….

YEARS 2-3

Coaching boys, ages seven to eight, playing coach-pitch and machine-pitch baseball was a leap in achievement for the players and coaches.

1. In addition to creating a fun experience, the coaches had a season goal of having every player be able to hit, throw, and catch.

2. Hitting practice consisted of eleven boys watching one batter. We didn't learn much from Year 1.

3. Throwing and catching practice consisted of sixty thrown balls and usually about twenty caught balls for each player. We learned that repetition matters and leads to improvement.

4. Victory was teaching players how to make outs on defense.

5. Pretty much everyone was engaged and had a good time. Well, one player still didn't want to be there. His parents were insistent—probably to the detriment of everyone else. He was a nice

boy, but quick to let everyone know his attendance was under protest.

6. Game scores were kept. The players did well at practice because they were motivated to do well in games. Bragging rights at school was a huge thing.

7. Biggest lessons learned: Keep the players constantly moving—doing stuff—and not watching. Introducing competition in practice kept players engaged and having fun. Bubble gum is a terrific prize for winning practice competitions.

If you are running a business that has clarity of mission and some semblance of a tactical execution plan, you probably see similarity between this team and your company. I'm guessing your company has some processes in place in certain areas and not so much in others. You probably got there by a bit of "hit and miss" where organized employees tended to create order and other employees who were more "seat of the pants" brought randomness and lack of focus toward achieving results.

YEAR 4

Coaching nine-year-old player pitch baseball was another significant leap in achievement for the players and coaches.

1. The coaches had a season goal of developing a strong team, where each player had a role that allowed him to contribute, feel valued, and be recognized for his achievement.

2. The concept of three practice stations was introduced. As an example, hitting, infield, and outfield stations were set up where players rotated every fifteen minutes. A coach worked each station, with four players at a time. Instruction was specific. Lots of

repetition produced amazing results—and players dramatically improved their skills.

3. Victory was teaching players how to become a team. I drafted a girl to be on the team. She was the only girl in the league. My idea was to teach the better players how to be leaders and make her feel welcome on a team comprised of boys while becoming a team contributor. My instincts were wrong. She turned out to be our best hitter and a major source of inspiration. The guys looked up to *her*—and she enjoyed being a team leader.

4. The biggest challenge as a board member was serving as a coach trying to build a healthy team culture in a league that was developing the culture it would soon grow into. With some other coaches and teams, the goal of winning at all costs superseded respect for the game, opponents, and teammates. As an example, when an opposing coach badgers a fourteen-year-old umpire into calling a game early so his team can win a playoff game, something is wrong, especially when parents on the opposing team are encouraging this behavior—quite vocally. Meanwhile, players on both teams sat in the infield and watched this all play out—much to their surprise. The players knew who won the game. But at the end of the day, did it really matter? After all, these were nine-year-old boys playing a game. On this particular day, the players were able to witness a few adults acting like spoiled children having temper tantrums. This behavior was the complete opposite of what we try to teach our young athletes.

5. Chemistry and culture were everything on this team. Everyone got better individually, and the players were surprised by how *good* they were at the end of season.

6. Biggest lessons learned: Everyone on the team was important. The weakest hitter on this team actually got the biggest hit in our last playoff game. The amount of cheering that went on at that moment just may have broken the sound barrier!

7. This year marked the beginning of a select baseball program that supplemented the Little League experience. The select team hardly won any games until season's end, when it won an end-of-summer tournament near the Canadian border. Hard work and humility ultimately resulted in a positive outcome—as measured by wins and losses.

Not only did the team coaches figure out that *Culture was Everything*, but they also began building a process around skill and team development. Skill development came from training stations, while team development came through building culture by recognizing and connecting individual achievement with team success. Does the experience of this baseball team sound like your company? The strong culture provides foundational support for systematizing process for individuals and the departments they work in.

YEARS 5-6

Coaching boys, ages ten and eleven, was the tipping point in developing a strong and vibrant baseball program.

1. The program invested in coach development. To become better, the program invested by sending coaches to professional clinics to develop their instructional skills in pitching, catching, fielding, and hitting.

2. Practice plans were developed and written down so skill and team development were logically sequenced throughout the course of a season.

3. Players were grouped according to relative skill, so each one was close enough in ability to create a competitive environment where players pushed each other to improve.

4. The select program found opportunities to participate in out-of-town tournaments at multiple age groups. These tournaments provided an opportunity to strengthen friendships and build community.

5. Higher levels of competition were consistently sought out, resulting in the teams and program dramatically elevating their game!

6. As a program, the ten-year-old All Star team won the State Title and the eleven-year-old All Star team took second place in the district tournament, losing in the finals to the eventual State champion.

Observing what top programs did—and emulating their success by employing best practices—enabled the Little League and select programs to take a giant leap forward from *Good to Great*. The program and teams were less about baseball and more about building friendship and community. Success was the outcome from deliberately moving toward high performance, and by focusing on the essential few, institutionalizing what worked, and discarding what was unimportant. If this description sounds like your company, you are way ahead of your competitors.

YEAR 7

Coaching twelve-year-old boys was perhaps the easiest year from a systems perspective—coaching templates for each practice were developed the prior year. Select players had the benefit of being on the same team for three years. Competition got tougher, but the results were consistent—this team won way more games than it lost. And the kids and families were having a great time.

1. The program continued to invest in coach development.

2. Practice plans were refined from the prior season.

3. Players were provided access to professional position instruction outside of the regular team practices.

4. The select team out-of-town experience provided a reward for lots of practice.

5. As a program, the Majors division All Star team won the State Title, Regional Championship, and made it to the Little League World Series in Williamsport, Pennsylvania. A second team of select ball players in the same age group competed in a national tournament in Cooperstown, the birthplace of baseball, the very same week.

The commitment of families and players, two teams deep, enabled this magical experience to play out during the middle of August, 2009. It was a good week for youth baseball on Mercer Island.

In summary, to develop a winning program and team, systematize what works and discard what doesn't. To systematize the entire season, create manuals, actively mentor, and develop a twelve week "practice and game plan" that can be replicated. Teach your coaches how to coach and build teams. Most importantly, build a strong culture that becomes institutionalized and survives annual changes in board leadership and coaching. By the way, the same principles apply for your business!

Little League Profile – Cameron Johnson

Systematizing process in a scalable way enabled Cameron Johnson to build businesses that produced ever increasing cash flows. Now twenty-seven years old, Cameron has owned and run small businesses for eighteen of those years.

In 1994 at age nine, Cameron launched his first home-based business by making invitations for his parents' holiday party. Two years later, he saved up several thousand dollars by selling greeting cards. His company was called Cheers and Tears.

In 1997, Cameron partnered with teen entrepreneurs, Aaron Greenspan and Tom Kho, to create a company called Surfingprizes.com, which through online advertising provided scrolling advertisements across the top of a user's web browser. Individuals who downloaded the software received twenty cents per hour, a tiny fraction of the value to the advertiser, in exchange for the inconvenience of having ads displayed across their computer screen.

To systematize their money-making machine, these young entrepreneurs used a classic multi-level marketing strategy to spread the service. Users who referred Surfingprizes.com to a new customer received 10 percent of that new person's hourly revenue.

Not content just to sell the software, the boys wanted a piece of the advertising revenue stream, by partnering with companies such as DoubleClick, L90, and Advertising.com, which could sell the ads for them. Under these agreements, the middlemen would collect 30 percent of any ad revenue sold, while the three boys split the remaining 70 percent, from which they paid any referral fees.

Cameron was quoted as saying, "I was fifteen years old and receiving checks between $300,000 and $400,000 per month." At age nineteen, he sold the company name and software to an undisclosed buyer, while retaining his customer database. Cameron also added, "Before my high school graduation, my combined assets were worth more than $1 million."

Cameron's advice to other entrepreneurs is, "Put yourself out there and don't be afraid of rejection. Don't be afraid to ask anything."

Systematizing Process—Business

Let's begin by identifying the costs of not systematizing your business:

Owner/CEO: If you are working all the time to keep things running, you have managed to create a high stress job for yourself that requires your constant active involvement. This business can't be sold for much money because a new owner will recognize that not much is sustainable if you are not working all the time.

A more valuable company will not miss having the old owner around, provided it is sustainable and runs like a solid business with strong leadership and teams with sound systems of sales/marketing, operations, and finance/administration.

In other words, superheroes are meant for comic books, not business. Becoming a metaphorical superhero who continually "saves the company" by working longer hours—to a physical and mental breaking point—doesn't make sense!

In fact, the opposite is most effective. Owners can increasingly build value through their *obsolescence*. How is that possible? Let's look at a hypothetical company that is profitable and operating under basic frameworks of good, better, and best:

Good: The business owner/executive is a superhero. He (or she) makes all decisions, major and minor. Nothing gets done without his approval. At some point, this company cannot grow because the owner simply runs out of capacity to manage decision-making. Conversely, the owner/executive becomes a hostage to his business because it cannot operate without his active involvement. The bigger his company gets, the more hours he has to work. Work is exhausting.

Better: The business owner recognizes he is a mere mortal and begins to develop leaders capable of building and running teams within the company while maintaining a strong and healthy culture. The owner is important to the company's success, but he is not essential to it functionally operating on a day-to-day basis. Ownership is rewarding because the company is thriving and the owner can actually get away from the business, take vacations, and find balance in his life.

Best: The business owner is a humble servant to a company that does not *need* the owner to be actively involved, regardless of whether or not the owner chooses to be involved. A true asset has been built—the company is valuable because it provides great value to customers or clients in an increasingly profitable manner and has employees who cannot imagine working anywhere else. As a result, dramatically increasing value in the business becomes inevitable.

In my opinion, many business owners would benefit from developing a long-term plan—*working toward* becoming obsolete. My question is: "Why wouldn't you want to own or run a business that profitably grew with increasing regularity while you increasingly had more time to do other things? If this scenario sounds desirable, why are you waiting to get started?

THE VALUE OF DISCRETIONARY TIME

Because this point is so important, I'll say the same thing another way. If you want to build *real* value in your life, start thinking about ways to increase *your* discretionary time. I'll share a quick example:

"Steve" is building a professional services firm. He and I recently had a conversation about his definition of success as it related to the firm. It went something like this:

Steve: Well…I certainly have revenue goals. And achieving this goal will mean success!

Me: Okay. Let's talk about that—and for the sake of discussion, we'll assume your personal revenue goal is $1 million per year. That number may be high or low for you, but now we have a basis for a conversation.

Steve: Makes sense to me. What do you want me to think about?

Me: You are missing a very important point about building value as it relates to your definition of success. I'll use an extreme example to illustrate. In order to accomplish your goals, what if you had to work 8,000 hours per year to earn $1 million? That essentially means you are working the equivalent of four full-time employees, or twenty-two hours per day, 365 days per year. In achieving financial success, answer these two questions: 1) What will you do with the remaining two hours each day? and 2) What was the cost to your family, health, happiness, and life for you to realize your financial goal?

Steve: Hey, that's a good point!

Me: Let's go to the other extreme and assume that you could find a way to earn $1 million per year and only work one hour in that year. With the additional 7,999 hours of discretionary time you now have, would you look at success differently?

Steve: I get it now—obtaining discretionary time is an important component to building value.

Me: Yes, and while you could choose to spend twenty-two hours per day in your business, I'm guessing there are better ways to live your life and give it meaning. Your family probably agrees with me!

The moral of the story: Value to the owner is created by increasing discretionary time. Too often, the focus is strictly on monetary goals. Don't get blinded by dollar signs.

By the way, the answer to solving this riddle is to build a firm that doesn't need you to be there all the time!

SYSTEMATIZE PROCESS

Discretionary time is captured when you build a system within your company to do what you are currently performing.

The value creation equation looks like:

Creating Business Processes and Procedures = More Discretionary Time

Sometimes, you have to invest in others, develop their talents, and think about how to create something that can survive without your active involvement before you can truly build value.

Said another way, a company's value increases the moment an owner can be extricated from a position integral to its success. Not having systems and processes that allow the company to grow profitably without the owner's active involvement will significantly devalue your business to a potential buyer.

This concept can and should be taken further throughout the company. If you want to take a significant step toward creating a more valuable business, build a company that can survive turnover at every position. Invest in developing your leaders and help them be successful in building teams within their departments.

By the way, when you have replicable systems and processes in place, regardless of the person doing the work, you have also reduced the risk of things going wrong and increased the likelihood that the business can grow in a scalable way without having your business unravel due to overworked employees (or an overworked owner!)

Systemization = lower risk

Sales

Marketing

Customer service

Operations

Finance

Accounting

Human resources

Information technology

Let's review key points before I give you a practice drill to work on.

1. Repeatable systems = sustainability.

2. Lack of repeatable systems = business risk.

3. To build value in your company, ensure that each area of the business is employing not only best practices, but also has documented processes and created systems of backup and redundancy so no individual solely carries the *keys of knowledge* in any part of your business. Examples might be: a Sales VP who is the only person who has a relationship with all the key customers, or the

head of Information Technology, who is the only person with *keys to the data systems* that feed sales, operations, and accounting.

Okay. Now it is time to continue writing in your game plan journal, and to answer the following questions to help develop systematized processes in your company:

Build an organization chart with job descriptions for each position:

_____

_____

Ask each department head to work with your Human Resources leader, or engage an outside professional to help get this done. Without a formal job description, it is hard to assign responsibility and accountability for work that is being done.

_____

_____

_____

_____

_____

_____

_____

_____

_____

_____

_____

_____

_____

Ask each department head to self-assess where risk exists in the company as it relates to:

1. Key business processes that are undocumented.

_____

_____

_____

_____

_____

2. Key tasks where only one person knows how to do the work.

_____

_____

_____

_____

_____

3. Employees who refuse to share knowledge on how to do their jobs.

_____

_____

_____

_____

_____

4. Key relationships with customers and vendors where only one person has the relationship.

_____

_____

_____

_____

_____

_____

_____

5. Employees who are reluctant to help build relationships between key customers/vendors with others in the company.

_____

_____

_____

_____

_____

_____

_____

With department head and respective employees:

1. Document key business processes. Documentation is complete and sufficient when others in the company can do the work without oversight.

---

2. Ensure that at least two employees in the company can do every task required within the company.

---

3. Coach employees who refuse to share knowledge on how to do their jobs. Help them recognize that business is a team sport. Keep team players, and find ways to shed individual performers who want to work solo.

---

4. In the same spirit, make sure key customers and vendors have at least two people in the company they know and want to work with, thus developing depth in your company's ability to serve these key people.

_____

_____

_____

_____

_____

_____

5. Coach employees who are reluctant to help build relationships between key customers/vendors with others in the company. Help them understand that business is a team sport. Find ways to shed individuals who want to work solo.

_____

_____

_____

_____

_____

_____

_____

Everything should be made as simple as possible, but not simpler.

— Albert Einstein

SCORING THE GAME

Can your business survive losses of key employees without significant damage to your company? If so, congratulations! You have increased the likelihood of repeatable success, year after year!

9th INNING SCORECARD

What are your key takeaways from this inning?

_____

_____

_____

_____

_____

_____

_____

_____

_____

_____

_____

_____

_____

_____

_____

_____

_____

Major League Profile – Henry Ford

Systematizing process comes from Henry Ford, who founded the Ford Motor Company and also invented the modern day assembly line of production for his Model T cars.

During his time, Ford was one of the richest people in the world. Today Ford Motor Company has dealerships all over the world, is one of the largest car manufacturers on the planet, and was the only U.S. auto manufacturer not to take federal bailout money during the financial crisis in 2008.

Ford started the Ford Motor Company with several investors. His company was known for paying its workers extraordinarily high wages for its time, enabling him to draw the talent and ability to support company operations. The company's breakthrough came upon introducing the Ford Model T, which was priced so low that the majority of American drivers soon were driving one.

Ford offered three leadership lessons:

1. **Value your employees:** If you demonstrate appreciation for each and every person on your team, you will attract employees without problem. More than just monetary compensation, employees want to work in an environment where they are valued and essential to the organization's success. Strive to give everyone on the team a sense of value. In the long run, great employees will continue to be drawn to your company.

2. **Self-belief is essential:** Your self-belief as a leader is infectious. Your willingness to strive toward the impossible will inspire your team members and push their limits to greatness.

   Ford had a very high level of self-belief and constantly encouraged his employees to push the limits of their imagination.

3. **We are created to do work:** Embrace the truth that work is a large part of life. The moment you decide to retire, your mind begins to deteriorate and your body begins to weaken.

Ford understood the importance of work and that people find fulfillment when they use the potential for greatness that lies within each of us. To Ford, retirement was never an option.

PART 4

....

Extra Innings

Hall of Fame Results

10th INNING

Building Advocacy and Relationships— Baseball

CREATING A REMARKABLE CUSTOMER EXPERIENCE

The Cooperstown Dreams Park experience is not just a national title baseball tournament; it is about your children, families, and the purity of the cultural life enrichment that it offers. Each year over 14,000 players become heroes.

The players, parents, brothers, sisters, grandparents, other family members, and friends all have ONE DREAM—to appreciate the purity of the game, to enjoy the experience of a lifetime, and to play baseball where it all began.

— Lou Presutti Jr. Founder, Cooperstown Dreams Park

If you wanted to create a thriving and sustainable youth baseball program that had a very high return rate of participants year after year, one strategy should be to deliver on the goal of creating a totally awesome experience for ALL involved. Lou Presutti Jr. and his team at Cooperstown Dreams Park deliver the gold standard for the remarkable and memorable experience in the world of youth-select level tournament baseball.

So what are the business results of having raving customers? Use Cooperstown Dreams Park as an example; the program is *extremely well run*, and every week, 1,200 players and 200 coaches have a very positive experience. As a result, select baseball programs send a new group of players the following year, and through word-of-mouth, demand for entrance into the tournament now exceeds available tournament slots. This tournament results in friendships being formed and relationships deepened. Parents join in and make the Cooperstown experience part of a memorable and once-in-a-lifetime experience. From a business perspective, it is pretty easy to see how Lou Presutti Jr. has created a thriving and sustainable program out of his grandfather's dream.

Now, let's for a minute assume that Cooperstown Dreams Park fell flat on its face in delivering a remarkable customer experience, and for a variety of reasons, the tournament was poorly run and everyone had an awful time. So bad in fact that NONE of the 1,200 teams attending in the current year decided to return the following season. In one short year, this enterprise would go from thriving to extinct.

This extreme example illustrates a very important point. The questions I ask you to consider are: Which tournament experience would you want your family to become involved with? Which tournament experience would you run away from, without looking back?

Now, use this analogy to think about the state of your business and how word-of-mouth, promises, trust, and relationships positively or negatively impact things like customer, vendor, and employee relationships, organizational sustainability, and overall profitability.

By the way, I and another coach took a team to Cooperstown Dreams Park during the week of August 15, 2009. Every now and then, when I run into players and parents who were part of that pilgrimage, we still talk about how great that trip was.... More importantly for Lou and his business, we are all advocates and a part of his brand by proactively talking to others about *why* they should try and get a tournament slot and be part of a unique and memorable experience.

THE REALIZATION OF A MISSION AND VISION

My favorite remembrances....

Going back to the 1st inning of this book, I talked about my two sons, Alex and Carl, and the hitting lesson given to them as six-year-olds back in 2002 by Ben Davis at the Seattle Mariners training facility in Peoria, Arizona. This lesson inspired both boys and ultimately took us all on a journey to Cooperstown and for a week-long baseball tournament.

On the final tournament day, Carl ended up hitting three home runs, two in a single game, with the second home run going so far it probably landed on the train going by and headed to New York City. After seven years, Carl realized his vision of hitting well in Cooperstown.

The night after our final game, our team took a trip into downtown Cooperstown and visited the National Baseball Hall of Fame and Museum. Surprisingly, while the parents enjoyed the trip, the players seemed to get bored after about an hour. I took this boredom to mean that the experience of a week-long tournament set a very high bar that couldn't being reached by seeing memorabilia from years gone by. We were indeed blessed.

After this visit, the players and parents presented both coaches with a small gift—a signed bat from all the players. The presentation ceremony was located at the exact spot where Babe Ruth, Ty Cobb, Honus Wagner, Christy Mathewson, and Walter Johnson were inducted into the National Baseball Hall of Fame in 1939. How cool is that?

Later that evening, Alex realized his vision of running the same bas-es as Babe Ruth when he, Carl, and I snuck over the fence at Abner Doubleday Field and spent a few minutes sitting in the dugouts and running around the bases. That was special....

My final memory is standing with Alex, looking out at the Catskill Mountains from a hill on the Cooperstown Dreams Park complex, in awe of the week we had just experienced. Alex turned to me and said, "Thanks, Dad, for being my coach all these years." In that moment, my vision was realized....

Little League Profile – Greyson MacLean

Building positive word-of-mouth and an army of advocates is what Greyson MacLean accomplished, after creating a new solution to an old problem and developing the proverbial "better mousetrap."

Greyson MacLean is thirteen years old and the creator of BrickStix, which makes static-cling decals and stickers for plastic building blocks such as Lego and Mega Bloks. As a young child, Greyson was always frustrated with the stickers that came with each Lego set. If he ever pulled a label off the block, a sticky residue remained on the plastic. If he left the label on, the brick was permanently labeled. This problem needed to be fixed.

In 2009 at age nine, Greyson found a UV label on the lens of a pair of sunglasses that was without adhesive. He tested the label on his bricks and the static-cling decal worked perfectly. This discovery was the basis for his new product and company, BrickStix, which he founded in 2010 and debuted in 2011 at Toy Fair in New York.

BrickStix decals are removable, reusable, and work with almost all plastic blocks. Greyson's family has invested about $20,000 into the business. Since the release in February 2011, BrickStix has sold more than 30,000 units and the company was profitable its first year.

Positive word-of-mouth has fueled success. MacLean has already appeared on *The Martha Stewart Show* and *Late Night with Conan O'Brien*. Additional accolades have helped, including Young Inventor of the Year from the 2011 Toy and Game Inventor Awards. BrickStix products are sold at over 300 stores in the U.S. and Canada and via the company website, BrickStix.com. International sales to Australia, Sweden, South Korea, and Japan are also fueling sales growth.

Greyson's goal was simply stated, "I wanted a way to customize my builds without ruining the bricks." He succeeded, and now others are proactively telling their friends to buy these products.

Building Advocacy and Relationships— Business

One way to build significant value in your company is to start moving customers/clients from shorter-term transactions to longer-term relationships with customers and partners who are your advocates. The difference in revenue generated, profits produced, and your company's value over time becomes astonishing!

Think of a transaction as one time, a relationship as an annuity, and an advocate as a super-relationship!

Let's work through a simple exercise to illustrate this point:

Assumptions:

1. New business: $1 million per year.

2. Customer/client turnover rate: 100 percent for transaction-driven business; 0 percent for relationship-driven business.

3. Building strong relationships with customers/clients over time will result in word-of-mouth advocacy that produces new business. This result usually doesn't happen in a turnover environment.

4. Period of time: five years.

Company A: transaction-driven revenue

1. Paul is a business development dynamo. He produces $1 million per year in new business.

2. For a combination of reasons, customers/clients do not stay with his company more than one year.

3. Paul replaces the revenue that leaves the door each year.

4. In the first five years, Company A generates $1 million in annual revenue.

Company B: relationship-driven revenue

1. Paula is also a business development dynamo. She also produces $1 million per year in new business.

2. The big difference is that Company B does not lose customers/clients—they never leave!

3. In the third year, customers/clients start talking to their friends and make referrals to Company B.

4. The revenue stream looks like this: Year 1 = $1 million, Year 2 = $2 million, Year 3 = $4 million, Year 4 = $6 million, and Year 5 = $8 million.

The Five-Year Difference:

1. Company A never grows.

2. Company B has developed long-term relationships with customers/clients that turn into an annuity-like revenue stream.

3. Company B's customer/client relationships resulted in referrals, which further increased revenue in Years 3-5.

4. Year 5 revenue is eight times higher in Company B than Company A.

Which company do *you* want to own? Obviously, the one that has developed relationship-driven and advocate-driven revenue! So, develop deep and lasting relationships with your customers/clients to build a valuable company....

Building trust and relationships with customers is a great way to build value in your company with dramatic results. Do the opposite by treating customers poorly and your company will move into the "Wheel of Pain," which reduces company profitability, any goodwill your business has with its customers, and ultimately, what your company is worth.

This is what the Wheel of Pain looks like:

1. Customers are unhappy.

2. You spend resources to save customers.

3. You lose customers.

4. Customers tell others of experience.

5. You spend more to acquire new customers.

6. Customers seek out your competitors.

7. Your resources get stretched—more customers become dissatisfied.

8. The cycle repeats.

When customers go out of their way to say bad things about your business to other people, you've got a big problem. Stopping the Wheel of Pain from spinning is difficult, not fun at all, and very expensive. This stuff happens all the time—if company culture and process permit!

Managing loss of customers can become a very expensive business problem. Remember:

Loyal customers = annuity like revenue

Advocate customers = ever increasing annuity like revenue

The inverse is also true!

So, what can you do to avoid The Wheel of Pain? First, clearly define "customer centric values" in your organization. If "customer first" is a strong value in your company, make sure only to hire employees who "get it"! Values become culture. The U.S. Postal Service has a culture in its organization. So does UPS.... Call me crazy, but I prefer UPS's culture to that of the U.S. Postal Service. If you have ever stood in line at the post office, I think you get my point!

A second observation is that as small businesses evolve and become larger companies, things like policies and procedures get implemented in order to systematize business processes and support growth. When this situation happens in your business, be sure to maintain focus on what's really important—serving customers and doing it well! The U.S. Postal Service has implemented tons of policies and processes over time. So has UPS.... Again, if you have ever stood in line at the post office, you get my drift. That's why strong and healthy culture (3rd inning) is needed to complement systematizing process (9th inning).

The most successful companies, regardless of size, understand how to keep long-term customers and maintain their "revenue annuity stream." Those who don't, do so at their peril....

WHAT IS THE PROCESS OF BUILDING ADVOCACY AND RELATIONSHIP?

Many strategies exist for how to build relationships and create raving fans who become your advocates. Blaine Millet, a friend, business and social media strategist, and a huge customer advocate, shared one of the best strategies with me. Blaine and his brother Gary wrote the book *Creating and Delivering Totally Awesome Customer Experiences*, which describes in detail how to have *raving* and *loyal* customers and create long-term relationships.

One important piece to remember is people talk about *experiences* more than a product or service. You can see this in dramatic fashion today on the social media networks. From what Blaine tells me, generally 75 percent of the conversation on social networks is about the *experience* people have with you and your company, not your specific product or service. To get feedback on how you are doing in pursuit of delivering an awesome experience, follow social networks and learn how customers, along with their friends and followers, talk about your company. Deliver a great customer experience and get people talking about it, and you will be on your way to building loyalty and advocates in the market.

Much of the content in this chapter came from Blaine's thinking and generous sharing with me. In their book, Blaine and Gary teach the reader a very specific process to deliver consistently and repeatedly a truly awesome customer experience. I am here to tell you it doesn't come from just telling your employees to "be nicer and friendlier" to your customers. If you want to build a "customer-centric" organization that creates both loyal customers and advocates, it takes work and a process. Blaine and Gary also created a very unique Promise Strategy, which specifically helps build and create advocates in a way that becomes part of the organization's culture and mission. To learn more, I encourage you to connect with Blaine on his social media channels and read his blogs. This will help you in your journey to build advocacy.

Below is a very short recap of how the Promise Strategy works:

1. Identify the promises you want to make to your customers and the ones you feel you can keep on a consistent basis.

2. Identify the promises you've made. Your new customer is essentially a transaction or series of short transactions.

3. Track how well you are keeping these promises on these transactions. Not keeping your promises means you don't get to the next step.

4. By keeping your promises, you will build trust.

5. By building trust, you will begin to create and build a strong relationship.

6. Relationships lead to loyalty, and loyalty is really a way to transform transaction or one time revenue into more of an annuity type stream of revenue.

7. Advocates come from loyal relationships where you absolutely thrill customers and they start proactively talking to others about you positively.

WHAT ARE POSSIBLE OUTCOMES FROM TRYING TO EXECUTE THE PROMISE STRATEGY?

Now let's take these six steps above and apply them to a pretty standard way of thinking about how customers view their experiences with your company.

Dissatisfied: If your customer is dissatisfied with his experience with your company, chances are your company fails at keeping its promises. That's pretty basic, but let me ask a few questions for you to think through:

- How do you know what promises are being made and how well your company is keeping its promises, whether they are explicit or implicit?

- Does your company have a strong *customer first* culture in place?

- Do you have employees or departments within your company that are not good at keeping their promises?

- How do you know promises aren't being kept, or are you unaware of what is *really* going on in your company from the customer's perspective?

Satisfied: If your customer is satisfied with your company's performance, chances are your company is doing an adequate job of keeping your promises. How do you feel about the word "adequate"? Is it a ringing endorsement of which you can be proud? Chances are a satisfied customer or client will stay with you until a better deal comes along; whether it is price, payment terms, or even something as simple as an invitation to an entertainment event hosted by your competitors. Being content with being adequate is, in my opinion, a very risky strategy, and it devalues a company immeasurably.

Loyal: If a customer or client is loyal to your company, congratulations! Chances are, loyalty was earned by developing a level of trust from keeping promises over time. This trust created the foundation for building a long-term relationship. A loyal customer will not get seduced by competitors offering a shiny bell or whistle such as an introductory discount, promises of better product or service, or any other sales pitch. You have earned annuity-like revenue based on a mutually beneficial business relationship. This loyalty doesn't mean your customer will share his experience with your company with others. In fact, it may be a very well-kept secret that frankly provides a disservice to both you and your customer's business network!

Advocate: Imagine if your customer truly understood *why* he does business with your company, clearly understands and appreciates the value it provides, and recognizes how his life is enhanced as a result of his relationship with your business. If this were the case, and the customer understood how you could provide similar value to others in need, why wouldn't he proactively connect you with such people? He would, in fact, be enriching the prospective new client and you, and in turn, he would receive thanks and appreciation for making the connection. This scenario is the definition of people helping other people to be successful while enriching lives.

WHAT IS ONE WAY TO ACCELERATE GETTING PEOPLE TO BECOME YOUR ADVOCATES?

Blaine Millet likes to ask, "What if you tell your customers or clients up-front when they are new to your business that your single most important goal in the relationship is to WOW them so they feel compelled actively and proactively to tell others about why they should do business with you?" That usually starts up a great conversation and sets a very positive tone and a high bar of performance for your business to strive toward reaching. By setting this expectation, your company will undoubtedly get feedback you otherwise may not get if your customer or client is less than thrilled. In setting the high bar for expectation, you often get there. And you have now set the stage for earning another advocate.

NOW THAT YOU HAVE ADVOCATES, WHAT DO YOU WANT THEM TO SAY ABOUT YOU?

As a reminder, advocates are people who *proactively* go about saying good things about you. That is a good thing. However, *what* they are saying about you is what's important. For instance, if you could magically have your advocates say exactly what you want about you, what would it be?

Hmmm…. If you struggle with what you would like said, go back to the 2nd inning and reread the discussion about why your customers buy from you. Your advocates should be saying things that tap into the emotional reasons why someone would want to do business with you, the incredible experience you provide, and also explain clearly the value you provide.

Let's use two examples of what a customer might say about you:

1. Jane is a great person. I like her a lot. She is a terrific attorney who is very smart. You should talk to her.

2. I didn't know what to do or where to turn. A disgruntled employee was suing my company and I had visions of losing everything I had worked hard to build. Jane was exactly the person I needed to help me successfully resolve this matter. She is an expert in the field of employee litigation matters. When owners have these types of problems, Jane is always responsive, a great listener, a terrific litigant, and she knows her stuff. You should call Jane immediately.

So, which version of advocacy would you want shared on your behalf? Clearly, the second example highlights an area of expertise, the emotional reasons why Jane was engaged, and provides a ringing endorsement that she knows how to serve clients well. What are you doing to equip your advocates to say things like this on your behalf?

HOW PASSION FOR YOUR WORK CAN CREATE REMARKABLE CUSTOMER EXPERIENCES

The ability to be remarkable lies within each of us. To be remarkable really means going the extra mile and always doing more than is expected. Imagine if everyone in your company treated customers and co-workers in this manner. What would it mean to those they served, and to them, to you, and your company?

So the question is: Are you and your employees seizing the opportunity or not? At this question's center is service, the heart of leadership.

If going the extra mile to provide exceptional service makes sense to you, what will you do tomorrow to help your company take a step in the right direction?

WHAT ADVOCACY LOOKS LIKE—A CUSTOMER'S POINT OF VIEW

Do your clients or customers proactively tell others *why* they buy your product or service, raving about how the experience was awesome? Costco has countless people all over the world doing just that—and your company would be well-served to be more like Costco—delivering great value and delighted customers—day after day!

More often than not, the cost of NOT being remarkable or exceptional is to be like everyone else—struggling to survive, working hard for little money, and seeing your company and life spinning in the wrong direction. Does this sound a little like you and your business?

On July 14, 2012, my wife Carrie and I hosted the Bell family's First Annual Summer Celebration deck party. About two dozen friends and family showed up and helped launch the summer BBQ season while watching the nighttime fireworks. I say "First Annual" because all the guests invited themselves back for next year. I'm sure they all wanted to come back for our great view and our company, but let me tell you why we have Costco to thank for the start of a new tradition....

Getting ready for the party consisted of me hopping in the car, making a pilgrimage to the ATM machine, and then to Costco. What did I buy? The real question is: What did I not buy? Purchases consisted of every possible food and drink item, the shirt on my back that I wore to the party, along with a bunch of other items I stuffed into the back of my car. Leaving the parking lot, my wallet was a lot lighter, but the smile on my face could light up the sky. Shopping was a great experience!

The party was a blast. Our friends Scott and Denise were the first to arrive and the last to leave. They both work at Costco. They brought as a gift a BBQ tool kit—from Costco. We laughed about how Costco rules. It became a topic of conversation throughout the evening. Everyone could relate and shared a story or two. Scott actually got up at the end of the evening to thank my wife and I for hosting such a wonderful party—and then thanked Costco for making it all possible. Stand-up comedians would do well to get the laugh Scott received. There is truth in humor!

Why do I share this story? Well, think about how cool it would be if your customers and clients talked about your company this way. Would that make a significant difference in the lives of you and your employees, and the value of your company? If so, what's holding you back from getting started at becoming more like Costco? Value is delivered in many ways. Figure out what your company's unique value proposition is; then become relentless in executing it.

WHAT HAVE YOU LEARNED?

Let's review key thoughts before I give you a practice drill to work on.

1. Transaction-driven revenue is one time.

2. Relationship-driven revenue is like an annuity.

3. Advocacy-driven revenue is like an annuity on steroids.

4. Building advocacy is a process, which starts by keeping your promises, earning trust, building relationships, and creating loyalty, which can be accelerated through advocacy.

5. Everyone can be remarkable. What are you doing to help make remarkability happen?

Okay. Now it is time to continue writing in your game plan journal and to answer the following questions to work on building advocacy and relationships in your company:

What are the promises being made?

_____

_____

_____

_____

_____

_____

_____

_____

_____

_____

_____

_____

_____

_____

_____

_____

_____

_____

_____

_____

Are these promises being kept?

_____

_____

_____

_____

_____

_____

_____

_____

_____

_____

_____

_____

_____

_____

_____

_____

_____

_____

Define the level of trust earned by your customers. How does it show up or not show up?

_____

_____

_____

_____

_____

_____

_____

_____

_____

_____

_____

_____

_____

_____

_____

_____

_____

_____

_____

What specific things are being done to build relationships with your customers?

_____

_____

_____

_____

_____

_____

_____

_____

_____

_____

_____

_____

_____

_____

_____

_____

_____

What necessary tools are you giving your customers so they can become your advocates?

Businesses that have increased their investment in the customer experience over the past three years report higher customer referral rates and greater customer satisfaction. Customers turn into advocates. Customer experience is the sum of all experiences a customer has with a supplier of goods or services, over the duration of their relationship with that supplier.

— *Nick Finck, User Experience Director, Deloitte Digital*

SCORING THE GAME

If you have successfully executed on the business strategy of building advocacy and relationships with your customers, employees, vendors, and other key stakeholders, then you will become a World Series winner in the game of business. Congratulations!

10ᵗʰ INNING SCORECARD

What are your key takeaways from this inning?

_____

_____

_____

_____

_____

_____

_____

_____

_____

_____

_____

_____

_____

_____

_____

_____

_____

_____

_____

Major League Profile – Sara Blakely

Hall of Fame results accurately characterize the Sara Blakely story. She is the world's youngest self-made female billionaire, and in 2012, she was named one of the 100 most influential people in the world by *Time* magazine. She achieved this success as a sole-owner of a privately held business, and to this day, she owns 100 percent of her company without ever taking any outside investment.

Blakely was twenty-nine when she invested her entire life savings of $5,000 to come up with something flattering to wear under her white slacks. After six months, the one-time Disney World ride greeter and door-to-door fax machine salesperson found her new line of shaping underwear, Spanx, named one of Oprah Winfrey's Favorite Things. Over the past twelve years, Blakely has taken Spanx from a one-product wonder sold out of her Atlanta apartment and grown it into a company valued at over $1 billion, with just under $250 million in annual revenues and net profit margins estimated at 20 percent.

The first step of Blakely's journey was to protect intellectual rights to the Spanx product. To keep costs down, she ended up doing the patent online. The patent was approved and she successfully trademarked the name SPANX online.

Using the Internet to find hosiery manufacturers, Blakely spent a lot of time trying to convince them to take on a small and undercapitalized start-up as a customer. Only one manufacturer took her up on the idea, explaining that "he had two daughters and admired her passion." The prototype took a year to perfect and product comfort was key.

Blakely wanted a catchy name for her product and knew from doing stand-up comedy that the "K" sound makes people laugh. The name SPANKS came out of the sky like a lightning bolt. After doing some research, she discovered that made-up names are easier to trademark so SPANX was born.

Blakely wanted a bold and edgy packaging look to match the catchy name. She went with bold colors and added the verbiage "must be legal" to the packaging, and added, "Don't worry, we've got your butt covered!"

Introducing the products to stores started at Neiman Marcus, when Blakely flew to Dallas and personally demonstrated the product, showing before and after looks while wearing her cream pants. Three weeks later, SPANX was being sold at Neiman Marcus. Blakely asked all of her friends to go to the stores, make a huge fuss over the product, and buy them up. SPANX quickly caught on. Blakely used the same process to have her product sold at Saks, Nordstrom, Bloomingdale's and other major retailers.

Zero advertising was spent to promote SPANX. Word-of-mouth fueled a new national craze. Sara did a year of in-store demonstrations, while also calling newspapers, magazines, and TV stations to get a lot of media coverage. The tipping point came when Sara and SPANX were featured on *The Oprah Winfrey Show*. She has also been on *The Today Show*, *The View*, *The Tyra Banks Show*, CNN, and countless other television programs and news channels, as well as in the pages of *Forbes*, *Fortune*, *People*, *Entrepreneur*, *In Style*, *The New York Times*, *USA Today*, *Glamour*, *Vogue*, and many more.

To broaden the reach of her product, Blakely negotiated a deal with Target to sell ASSETS with the idea that all women deserve the opportunity to make the most of their assets.

To give back, a portion of all SPANX and ASSETS purchases go to the Sara Blakely Foundation, which was originally funded by a $750,000 gift from Sir Richard Branson, whom Sara met while appearing on a reality-based TV show called *The Rebel Billionaire*. This foundation focuses on supporting and empowering women around the world to follow their dreams.

When asked about the single best business lesson she ever learned, Blakely shared a story about how her father encouraged failure. She was quoted as saying, "We'd come home from school and at dinner he'd say: 'What did you fail at today?' And if there was nothing, he'd be disappointed. It was a really interesting kind of reverse psychology. I would come home and say that I tried out for something and I was just horrible and he high-fived me."

Blakely offers two leadership lessons:

1. **Believe in yourself:** If you know your product or service is compelling, then confidence and perseverance will carry you through difficult times when others do not share your enthusiasm.

2. **It is okay to fail:** Failure comes from taking risk and all successful businesses need to take risk and accept failure as part of the growing process.

A FINAL NOTE

Now What?

In this book, you have learned that building value and wealth through your business comes from applying ten principles to your company:

1. **Defining Success:** Build a mission statement and personal vision for your company's future. Involve all key stakeholders in this conversation and build alignment of this mission and vision.

2. **Answering "Why?":** Identify your company's unique value proposition—and why customers choose to buy or not to buy from your business.

3. **Defining Culture and Values:** Invest the time to define and institutionalize the culture and values that bind your employees together in service to customers.

4. **Leaders and Teams:** Inspire followership to be a great leader. Work toward building strong leaders and teams.

5. **Developing Strategy and Tactically Executing the Plan:** Identify the essential few things that will move your company toward your definition of success. Develop a tactical plan for each strategic initiative and assign accountability and collaboration partners responsible for execution.

6. **Creating Alignment:** To accelerate the time it takes to achieve success, build alignment in your company's culture, strategy, and tactics from the top to bottom of your organization chart.

7. **Developing and Protecting Your Assets:** To build sustainably great outcomes, identify and protect the assets that produce value in your company. During this process, also take the time to eliminate non-performing assets.

8. **All About Risk:** Invest the time to identify all of your business risks and place them into five categories for how to deal with them. Then finish the work by preventing, managing, insuring, ignoring each risk, or developing a crisis management plan.

9. **Systematizing Process:** Build an organization chart with job descriptions. Have each department head assess where business risk lies in his or her respective area. Document key business processes and make sure teams are formed to get work done, both internally and externally.

10. **Building Advocacy and Relationships:** To increase revenue dramatically, build relationships that produce loyal annuity type revenue. Supercharge this revenue by turning your customers into advocates who tell others why they should do business with you.

Hopefully, you have come to the conclusion that realizing your dreams through business ownership is very achievable. Now it is time for the *rubber to meet the road*. You can read all of the "How To" books in the world, but unless you apply what you learn, you will never achieve your potential.

I would like to challenge you to follow Nike's motto of "Just Do it." Complete all of the exercises in this book—and transform Little League principles into Major League profits for your company!

My final request is for you to e-mail me at earl@islandcrestconsult-ing.com with the most inspirational moment you found in this book. In exchange for your feedback, I will offer you a complimentary fif-teen-minute consultation.

Your coach,

BONUS MATERIAL
Investing Time—The Third Choice

We all have time to spend or waste and it is our decision what to do with it. But once passed, it is gone forever.
— Bruce Lee

Regarding time, most people think in terms of it being spent or wasted. I'll offer a third idea—that *investing time* to improve your business is a much better alternative than spending or wasting it. By my definition, time well-invested produces a significantly improved business outcome and a dramatic reduction in future time spent.

So what does investing time look like? Using principles from this book, I'll offer five ideas to get you started:

1. Defining strategy and direction.

2. Developing effective leaders and teams.

3. Learning whom you can trust, determining why you can't trust some, and getting rid of those you cannot trust or develop to the point they can be trusted.

4. Empowering others to make decisions.

5. Creating systems of accountability and holding people accountable for their performances.

So what are the outcomes of investing time in these areas?

1. Clear direction provides goals and purpose for your leaders and teams. The absence of strategy and direction results in chaos.

2. Effective leaders and teams successfully execute strategy and direction.

3. Working with those you trust accelerates decision-making and reduces second-guessing.

4. Empowering others to make minor decisions keeps you focused on making the essential big decisions and keeps you out of the proverbial weeds that become a huge waste of your time.

5. Accountability enables everyone to understand where results and failures come from. Most people want to be held accountable and rewarded for results—but not always. The kindest thing you can do is to help some employees leave your company; this act also will benefit the excellent employees who stay.

Many other ways exist to invest time in your business. Take the time to figure out what this looks like. My goal is to get you thinking about time in a different way.

I challenge you to be proactive and invest thirty to sixty minutes every day in ways that will enable your business to grow and flourish. Each hour invested will improve business outcomes and save countless hours later spent undoing bad decisions resulting from not investing the time necessary to run your business wisely!

BONUS MATERIAL
Power of Persistence—The 212th Degree

The *power of persistence* is what enables ordinary people to achieve extraordinary results. The *lack of persistence* is what enables ordinary people to achieve ordinary results. I call this difference the 212th degree.

Water boils at 212 degrees Fahrenheit, the tipping point at which a liquid becomes a gas. In business and life, will you persist to reach the metaphorical *boiling point* in achieving your goals? If not, what's stopping you?

Achieving professional and personal goals and objectives is not guaranteed nor time certain. Because of this uncertainty, people often give up on their aspirations; sometimes just before a goal could have been reached. Does this happen to you and your business? What about in life?

In this book's 1st inning, I shared a great story about persistence when Ben Davis, catcher for the Seattle Mariners, gave a mini-hitting lesson and incredibly inspiring message to my six-year-old sons, Carl and Alex. Ben offered a quick tutorial on what it took to become a world-class hitter and end up as a hall of fame player. With a twinkle in his eye, Ben told Carl to close his eyes before swinging the bat, saying, "It works for me every time!" Carl obviously missed the joke, but he was nevertheless hooked on baseball and commenced his journey with a passion for becoming a great hitter.

Through six seasons, starting with T-ball, and progressing through Little League and Select baseball, Carl often struggled as a hitter, but he was one of the hardest working kids on my teams. The kid simply never gave up! On the final tournament day when he played at Cooperstown, Carl came into his own as a hitter, crushing three home runs, one of which is still probably orbiting the earth. It was amazing to watch and I couldn't have been more proud or happy for Carl that day. He came to realize the power of persistence.

So here is my challenge to you: Take some time to figure out what's really important—and then commit to persistence in achieving those goals. Embrace the challenges that business and life give you, and have a game plan for overcoming these adversities. Know the strengths and weaknesses of yourself, your company, and employees, never give up, begin with the end in mind, and have a systematic program in place for achieving your vision. Finally, become successful by helping others become successful.

ABOUT THE AUTHOR

Earl Bell is an author, professional keynote speaker, and the principal and founder of Island Crest Consulting. His coaching and consulting work with owners and executives helps them to realize their dreams. Earl teaches business owners how to reduce the time it takes to improve probability while dramatically increasing the company's value. His clients learn how to increase their personal income substantially while attaining the true measure of wealth—additional discretionary time to pursue their passions. Today, his clients' cumulative scorecard exceeds $230 million in shareholder wealth, multi-millions in personal income, and most importantly, not a lot of overtime at work.

Earl's career in the corporate world included roles as Chief Financial Officer and owner with several small to mid-sized companies throughout North America.

Earl's personal passion is youth sports, and he has coached twenty-eight teams since 2002. His interest in service to non-profits includes being a past Board Chair of Leadership Eastside and a past member of the Mercer Island Boys & Girls Club advisory board.

Earl grew up in Anchorage, Alaska, graduated from Seattle University, and lives on Mercer Island, Washington with his wife Carrie and three children, Alex, Carl, and Cara.

To learn more about Earl or to subscribe to his weekly Monday Morning Message, please visit his website at www.earlbell.com and check out his video channel at www.earlbell.tv

BOOK EARL BELL TO SPEAK AT YOUR NEXT EVENT

When it comes to choosing a speaker for your next event, you'll find no one more passionate and inspiring than Earl Bell when it comes to sharing stories about leadership, team building, navigating through change, and what it takes to be successful in business.

Whether your audience is 10 or 10,000, in North America or abroad, Earl Bell can customize an inspiring message that will leave your audience members ready to go back to their companies and *get things done*—with intent and purpose—and by design, not chance!

Earl Bell's style of speaking is to share stories with passion and humor and to inspire ordinary people to achieve extraordinary results.

www.earlbell.com

earl@islandcrestconsulting.com

(206) 420-5946